Southern Living

QUICK START

Homemade

Southern Living
QUICK START
Homemade

TIME-SAVING · BUDGET-FRIENDLY · EASY & DELICIOUS

Oxmoor House®

4

Hungry Yet?
This mouthwateringly delicious Grilled Chicken Tequila Burger on page 197 takes burgers to a new level!

Let's make dinner!

Bright, fun, and packed with over 180 great Southern recipes, *Quick Start Homemade* is your supermarket companion to help you get dinner on the table easier, faster, and for less money. Organized by main ingredients that stretch the dollar, these recipes let you cook with what you have on hand and with what's on sale, truly making it the smart way to shop for and make dinner.

First, get your kitchen stocked using our helpful guides on pages 6–9 so you're ready to cook up a flavorful meal anytime.

Next, check out these fantastic features on every recipe that make cooking with *Quick Start Homemade* even easier:

BUDGET-FRIENDLY MAIN INGREDIENTS
We've picked eight of the best, cost-saving main ingredients and devoted whole chapters full of great recipes to them.

QUICK TIPS
These clever ideas show you the best ways to get dinner on the table faster and simpler.

EASY SIDES
Round out your meal with simple shortcut side dishes paired with almost every recipe.

MAKE AHEADS
Prepare your meal in advance, so you can whip up a great meal, even on a hectic evening.

Stocked and Ready

When your pantry is organized with all the essentials, your kitchen is ready to start cooking whenever you are!

1. SPICES

Keep a variety of spices on hand like cumin, bay leaves, cinnamon, cayenne pepper, chili powder, ginger, paprika, peppercorns, kosher and table salt, and dried herbs.

2. OILS AND VINEGARS

Don't get tripped up by not having these pantry essentials at the ready: canola oil, vegetable oil, olive oil, sesame oil, and cooking spray, plus balsamic vinegar, cider vinegar, and red and white wine vinegar.

3. DRIED PASTAS

These staples keep indefinitely in airtight containers, so it's best to have a good variety of spaghetti, farfalle, penne, macaroni, couscous, and rice noodles, to name a few.

4. CANNED GOODS

More than just soup, canned goods like diced tomatoes, tomato sauce and paste, beans, vegetables, and fruits are a great way to add a little variety to dinner without planning ahead.

5. DRIED GRAINS AND LEGUMES

These cost-saving starches can turn chicken or a few vegetables into a meal, so stock up on dried beans, rice, barley, oats, and lentils.

6. BROTH

Vegetable broth, chicken broth, turkey broth, and beef broth are all great ways to add low-fat, rich flavor to soups, sauces, and more. Try cooking your pasta or rice in broth instead of water.

Jump-Start Ingredients

These easy add-ins are our favorite tricks for getting a flavorful dinner on the table even faster and without any extra effort.

SPICE BLENDS

Try mixing in a little curry, using Creole seasoning as a rub, or sprinkling Italian seasoning into pasta.

JARRED PASTA SAUCE

With tons of flavor combinations to pick from, jarred pasta sauce gives you all the flavor of daylong simmering, without the hassle.

REFRIGERATED PESTO

Creamier and brighter in color than the jarred shelf-stable version, use as a sauce or stir into soups and pastas for a jolt of fresh basil, Parmesan, and pine nut flavor.

CANNED BEANS

It couldn't get any quicker! They require no cooking—just toss into salads, casseroles, soups, and stir-fries.

SHREDDED CHEESE

Skip the cutting board and the grater with preshredded cheese. Look for cheese blends like Mexican blend—perfect for tacos or melty enchiladas.

BOTTLED DRESSING

Super versatile, there's more to dressing than salads! Use as a marinade, a light pasta sauce, or toss with vegetables before roasting.

PRECHOPPED VEGETABLES

Look for prepped onions, peppers, broccoli, carrots, zucchini, and more in the produce section or freezer aisle to speed up any recipe.

TOASTED NUTS

Buy them already toasted or toast-and-freeze for a quick and easy way to add crunch and protein to any dish.

CONTENTS

114 **Rotisserie Chicken**

From salads to casseroles, rotisserie chicken makes dinner a cinch and gives any dish from-scratch flavor.

142 **Chicken Breasts**

Buy chicken breasts in bulk when they're on sale, and use them up with this great mix of recipes from soups and kabobs to stir-fry and sandwiches.

168 **Pork Loin and Chops**

Versatile and flavorful, pork chops and tenderloins are not only a great source of lean protein, but they are a great way to stretch your dollar.

194 **Ground Meat**

Ground chicken, beef, and turkey are for more than just making burgers! Try a meaty chili, a hearty casserole, or a loaded tostada for delicious weeknight suppers.

1 PASTA

From orecchiette and ziti to egg noodles and spaghetti, you're sure to find a hearty pasta dinner the whole family will love.

GREEN BEAN PASTA SALAD WITH LEMON-THYME VINAIGRETTE, PAGE 36 ▶

Tortellini-and-Tomato Salad

MAKES 6 SERVINGS   **HANDS-ON TIME** 20 MIN.   **TOTAL TIME** 20 MIN.

- 2 (9-oz.) packages refrigerated cheese-filled tortellini
- ½ cup olive oil
- ½ cup freshly grated Parmesan cheese
- 3 Tbsp. fresh lemon juice
- 2 garlic cloves
- 1 tsp. Worcestershire sauce
- ½ tsp. table salt
- 2 cups baby heirloom tomatoes, halved
- 1 cup fresh corn kernels
- ½ cup thinly sliced green onions
- ½ cup coarsely chopped fresh basil

1. Prepare pasta according to package directions.

2. Meanwhile, process olive oil and next 5 ingredients in a blender until smooth. Toss olive oil mixture with hot cooked tortellini, tomatoes, and next 3 ingredients. Add salt and pepper to taste.

QUICK TIP Try using leftover grilled corn cut fresh off the cob to add even more summery flavor to this pasta.

easy side

Italian-Seasoned Bread: Preheat oven to 350°. Split 1 (12-oz.) French bread loaf lengthwise, and brush cut sides with ½ cup melted butter. Top with 6 garlic cloves, pressed; 1 tsp. dried oregano; and ½ tsp. dried parsley flakes. Bake until lightly browned and crisp.

Broccoli, Grape, and Pasta Salad

MAKES 6 TO 8 SERVINGS **HANDS-ON TIME** 25 MIN.
TOTAL TIME 3 HOURS, 30 MIN.

If you're a fan of broccoli salad, you'll love the combination of these colorful ingredients.

- ½ (16-oz.) package farfalle (bow-tie) pasta
- 1 lb. fresh broccoli
- 1 cup mayonnaise
- ⅓ cup sugar
- ⅓ cup diced red onion
- ⅓ cup red wine vinegar
- 1 tsp. table salt
- 2 cups seedless red grapes, halved
- 1 cup chopped toasted pecans
- 8 cooked bacon slices, crumbled

1. Prepare pasta according to package directions.

2. Meanwhile, cut broccoli florets from stems, and separate florets into small pieces using tip of a paring knife. Peel away tough outer layer of stems, and finely chop stems.

3. Whisk together mayonnaise and next 4 ingredients in a large bowl; add broccoli, hot cooked pasta, and grapes, and stir to coat. Cover and chill 3 hours. Stir pecans and bacon into salad just before serving.

QUICK TIP Cook the pasta al dente so it's firm enough to hold together when tossed with the tangy-sweet salad dressing.

make ahead

Prepare pasta as directed without adding pecans and bacon. Chill 3 hours or up to 1 day. Stir in pecans and bacon just before serving.

Sweet Chili-Lime Noodles with Vegetables

MAKES 1 SERVING   **HANDS-ON TIME** 20 MIN.
TOTAL TIME 25 MIN., INCLUDING SWEET CHILI-LIME SAUCE

- 1 cup cooked whole grain spaghetti (2 oz. uncooked)
- 2 cups shredded bok choy*
- ¼ cup grated carrot
- ¼ cup fresh snow peas
-    Sweet Chili-Lime Sauce
- ¼ cup shredded cooked chicken (optional)

1. Place pasta, next 4 ingredients, and, if desired, chicken in a medium-size microwave-safe plastic container. Cover with lid, and shake to combine.

2. Lift 1 corner of lid to allow steam to escape. Microwave at HIGH 2 minutes or until vegetables are tender.

2 cups shredded coleslaw mix or shredded cabbage may be substituted.

Note: We tested with Mueller's Whole Grain Spaghetti.

Sweet Chili-Lime Sauce

MAKES 3 TBSP.   **HANDS-ON TIME** 5 MIN.   **TOTAL TIME** 5 MIN.

- 2 Tbsp. bottled sweet chili sauce
- 2 tsp. lime juice
- ½ tsp. fresh grated ginger
- ¼ tsp. minced garlic

Stir together all ingredients until blended.

QUICK TIP Pack up this pasta as a satisfying lunch with some steamed edamame.

make ahead

Prepare noodles as directed through Step 1. Cover and chill up to 1 day. Continue with recipe as directed when ready to serve.

Skillet Ziti

MAKES 8 SERVINGS   **HANDS-ON TIME** 20 MIN.   **TOTAL TIME** 30 MIN.

- 8 oz. uncooked ziti pasta
- 1 lb. ground round
- 1 (10-oz.) package frozen chopped onion, thawed and drained well
- ½ tsp. table salt
- ¼ tsp. freshly ground black pepper
- 1 (26-oz.) jar tomato and basil pasta sauce
- 1 (8-oz.) container sour cream
- ⅓ cup (1½ oz.) shredded Parmesan cheese
- 1 (8-oz.) package shredded Italian six-cheese blend

1. Cook pasta according to package directions. Drain and set aside.

2. While pasta cooks, cook beef, onion, salt, and pepper in a large skillet over medium-high heat, stirring until beef crumbles and is no longer pink; drain.

3. Stir in pasta sauce; cook 1 minute or until thoroughly heated. Add pasta, stirring to coat.

4. Combine sour cream and Parmesan cheese. Stir into pasta mixture. Sprinkle Italian cheese blend over pasta mixture. Cover, reduce heat to medium, and cook 5 minutes or until cheese melts.

QUICK TIP This ziti dish cooks up twice as fast as the traditional oven-baked version—plus, it's creamier and cheesier.

easy side

Spinach-Parmesan Salad: Toss together 1 (10-oz.) package fresh spinach; 1 medium-size red onion, thinly sliced; 2 hard-cooked eggs, chopped; 1 cup garlic-seasoned croutons; and 2 Tbsp. grated Parmesan cheese. Serve with bottled dressing.

Roquefort Noodles

MAKES 6 TO 8 SERVINGS **HANDS-ON TIME** 20 MIN. **TOTAL TIME** 20 MIN.

Don't skimp on the quality of the blue cheese in this recipe—its bold flavor brings this dish to life.

1 (12-oz.) package wide egg noodles

1 Tbsp. jarred chicken soup base

½ tsp. olive oil

½ cup butter

6 to 8 green onions, sliced

4 to 6 oz. Roquefort or other blue cheese, crumbled

1 (8-oz.) container sour cream

Seasoned pepper

1. Cook noodles according to package directions, adding chicken soup base and oil to water.

2. Meanwhile, melt butter in a large heavy skillet over medium heat. Add onions, and sauté 5 to 7 minutes or until tender. Reduce heat to medium-low, and stir in Roquefort cheese, stirring constantly until cheese is melted. Remove from heat, and stir in sour cream until blended and smooth.

3. Toss together Roquefort cheese sauce and hot cooked egg noodles. Add seasoned pepper to taste.

> **QUICK TIP** By adding chicken soup base to noodles as they boil, this pasta packs more flavor than traditional egg noodles.

easy side

Lemon-Pepper Broccoli: Cook 2 (10-oz.) packages frozen broccoli spears in butter sauce according to package directions. Toss broccoli with ½ tsp. grated lemon zest and ¼ tsp. freshly ground black pepper.

Linguine with Sun-Dried Tomatoes

MAKES 6 SERVINGS　**HANDS-ON TIME** 16 MIN.　**TOTAL TIME** 26 MIN.

1　(16-oz.) package linguine

1　(7-oz.) jar sun-dried tomatoes in oil

¼　cup pine nuts

3　garlic cloves, minced

¼　cup extra virgin olive oil

1　(4-oz.) package crumbled feta cheese

2　Tbsp. thin fresh basil strips

1. Prepare pasta according to package directions.

2. Drain tomatoes, reserving 2 Tbsp. oil. Cut tomatoes into thin strips.

3. Heat pine nuts in a large nonstick skillet over medium-low heat, stirring often, 5 minutes or until toasted and fragrant. Remove nuts from skillet.

4. Increase heat to medium, and sauté garlic in 2 Tbsp. reserved oil and olive oil in skillet 1 minute or until garlic is fragrant. Stir in tomatoes, and remove from heat.

5. Toss together tomato mixture, hot cooked pasta, feta cheese, and basil in a large bowl. Sprinkle with toasted pine nuts.

QUICK TIP If you don't have linguine on hand, try substituting angel hair pasta or thin spaghetti.

try this twist

Linguine with Tuna and Sun-Dried Tomatoes:

Prepare recipe as directed. Stir in 2 (6-oz.) aluminum foil pouches solid white tuna chunks, drained, and 1 (3-oz.) can sliced black olives, drained.

Fresh Vegetable Lasagna

MAKES 8 SERVINGS   **HANDS-ON TIME** 30 MIN.   **TOTAL TIME** 3 HOURS, 14 MIN.

- 4 medium zucchini, halved lengthwise and thinly sliced (about 1½ lb.)
- 1 (8-oz.) package sliced fresh mushrooms
- 2 garlic cloves, minced
- Vegetable cooking spray
- 1 medium-size red bell pepper, chopped
- 1 medium-size yellow bell pepper, chopped
- 1 yellow onion, chopped
- ½ tsp. table salt
- 1½ cups ricotta cheese
- 1 large egg
- 2 cups (8 oz.) shredded part-skim mozzarella cheese, divided
- ½ cup freshly grated Parmesan cheese, divided
- 5 cups marinara sauce
- 1 (8-oz.) package no-boil lasagna noodles
- Garnish: fresh basil leaves

1. Preheat oven to 450°. Bake zucchini, mushrooms, and garlic in a jelly-roll pan coated with cooking spray 12 to 14 minutes or until vegetables are crisp-tender, stirring halfway through. Repeat procedure with bell peppers and onion. Reduce oven temperature to 350°. Toss together vegetables and salt in a bowl.

2. Stir together ricotta cheese, egg, 1½ cups shredded mozzarella cheese, and ¼ cup grated Parmesan cheese.

3. Spread 1 cup marinara sauce in a 13- x 9-inch baking dish coated with cooking spray. Top with 3 noodles, 1 cup sauce, one-third of ricotta mixture, and one-third of vegetable mixture; repeat layers twice, beginning with 3 noodles. Top with remaining noodles and 1 cup sauce. Sprinkle with remaining ½ cup shredded mozzarella and ¼ cup grated Parmesan cheese.

4. Bake, covered, at 350° for 45 minutes. Uncover and bake 10 to 15 more minutes or until cheese is melted and golden. Let stand 10 minutes.

Note: We tested with Ronzoni Oven Ready Lasagna Noodles.

QUICK TIP If there is any liquid in the vegetable mixture after roasting, drain it off before tossing with salt in Step 1.

make ahead

Prepare recipe through Step 3; cover and refrigerate up to 1 day. Bake, covered, at 350° for 55 minutes and uncovered for 10 to 15 more minutes.

Four-Cheese Macaroni

MAKES 8 SERVINGS   **HANDS-ON TIME** 40 MIN.   **TOTAL TIME** 1 HOUR, 15 MIN.

- 12 oz. cavatappi pasta or macaroni
- ½ cup butter
- ½ cup all-purpose flour
- ½ tsp. ground red pepper
- 3 cups milk
- 2 cups (8 oz.) freshly shredded white Cheddar cheese
- 1 cup (4 oz.) freshly shredded Monterey Jack cheese
- 1 cup (4 oz.) freshly shredded fontina cheese
- 1 cup (4 oz.) freshly shredded Asiago cheese
- 1½ cups soft, fresh breadcrumbs
- ½ cup chopped cooked bacon
- ½ cup chopped pecans
- 2 Tbsp. butter, melted

1. Preheat oven to 350°. Prepare pasta according to package directions.

2. Meanwhile, melt ½ cup butter in a Dutch oven over low heat; whisk in flour and ground red pepper until smooth. Cook, whisking constantly, 1 minute. Gradually whisk in milk; cook over medium heat, whisking constantly, 6 to 7 minutes or until milk mixture is thickened and bubbly. Remove from heat.

3. Toss together Cheddar cheese and next 3 ingredients in a medium bowl; reserve 1½ cups cheese mixture. Add remaining cheese mixture and hot cooked pasta to sauce, tossing to coat. Spoon into a lightly greased 13- x 9-inch baking dish. Top with reserved 1½ cups cheese mixture.

4. Toss together breadcrumbs and next 3 ingredients; sprinkle over cheese mixture.

5. Bake at 350° for 35 to 40 minutes or until bubbly and golden brown.

QUICK TIP Be sure to grate the cheeses yourself—they'll melt more easily and create a creamier dish.

easy side

Vinegar Tomatoes: Drizzle sliced fresh tomatoes with bottled oil-and-vinegar dressing; season with salt and pepper to taste.

make ahead

Prepare recipe as directed through Step 3; cover and chill for up to 1 day. Uncover and continue with recipe as directed, baking 10 to 15 more minutes, if necessary.

Sautéed Shrimp and Fettuccine

MAKES 4 SERVINGS   **HANDS-ON TIME** 10 MIN.   **TOTAL TIME** 20 MIN.

Whip up this restaurant-worthy dish in only 20 minutes!

¼ **cup butter**

1 **(0.7-oz.) envelope Italian dressing mix**

1 **lb. peeled and deveined medium-size raw shrimp**

1 **(9-oz.) package refrigerated fettuccine**

1. Melt butter in a large skillet over medium heat; stir in dressing mix. Add shrimp; cook, stirring constantly, 3 to 5 minutes or until shrimp turn pink.

2. Prepare pasta according to package directions. Serve shrimp immediately over pasta.

QUICK TIP Put the pasta on to cook as you start the shrimp to have dinner on the table in record time.

easy side

▶ **Sautéed Garlic Spinach:** Heat 1 Tbsp. olive oil in a Dutch oven over medium heat. Add 3 garlic cloves, thinly sliced, and cook 1 minute or until golden. Add 1 (6-oz.) package fresh baby spinach and cook 1 minute, turning with tongs. Add another 6-oz. package fresh baby spinach; cook, turning with tongs, 1 minute or until spinach wilts. Stir in ¼ tsp. freshly ground black pepper.

Grilled Chicken-and-Veggie Tortellini

MAKES 4 SERVINGS   **HANDS-ON TIME** 16 MIN.   **TOTAL TIME** 32 MIN.

This hearty Italian entrée features grilled chicken and zucchini tossed with store-bought cheese tortellini, pesto, chopped tomatoes, and Italian herb seasoning.

> 4   small zucchini, cut in half lengthwise (about 1 ¼ lb.)
> 2   skinned and boned chicken breasts (13 oz.)
> 1   Tbsp. freshly ground Italian herb seasoning
> 1   (19-oz.) package frozen cheese-filled tortellini
> 1   (7-oz.) container refrigerated reduced-fat pesto
> 2   large tomatoes, seeded and chopped
> Garnish: grated Parmesan cheese

1. Preheat grill to 300° to 350° (medium) heat. Sprinkle zucchini and chicken with seasoning.

2. Grill zucchini, covered with grill lid, 6 to 8 minutes on each side or until tender. At the same time, grill chicken, covered with grill lid, 5 to 6 minutes on each side or until done. Remove from grill; let stand 10 minutes.

3. Meanwhile, prepare pasta according to package directions.

4. Coarsely chop chicken and zucchini. Toss pasta with pesto, tomatoes, chicken, and zucchini. Serve immediately.

Note: We tested with McCormick Italian Herb Seasoning Grinder.

QUICK TIP For an easy twist, substitute frozen mushroom-filled tortellini or sun-dried tomato pesto.

easy side

▶ **Mixed Greens with Dijon:** Whisk together 1 Tbsp. balsamic vinegar, 1 Tbsp. olive oil, 1 tsp. honey, ¼ tsp. Dijon mustard, and ⅛ tsp. coarsely ground pepper in a large bowl until blended. Add 4 cups mixed salad greens; toss gently. Sprinkle with ½ cup red seedless grape halves.

Marinated Greek-Style Pasta

MAKES 14 TO 16 SERVINGS   **HANDS-ON TIME** 30 MIN.   **TOTAL TIME** 2 HOURS, 40 MIN.

This big-batch pasta salad is great for parties. Leftovers are perfect for next-day lunches straight from the fridge.

1   (16-oz.) package orecchiette pasta*
½   lb. hard salami slices, cut into strips
¼   lb. assorted deli olives, pitted, drained, and cut in half
1   (7-oz.) jar roasted red bell peppers, drained and chopped
6   pepperoncini salad peppers, cut in half lengthwise
½   English cucumber, thinly sliced into half moons
1½   cups bottled Greek vinaigrette with feta cheese, divided
1   pt. grape tomatoes, cut in half
¼   cup firmly packed fresh flat-leaf parsley leaves
4   oz. feta cheese, crumbled

1. Cook pasta according to package directions; drain. Rinse with cold running water.

2. Toss together pasta, salami, and next 4 ingredients. Add 1 cup vinaigrette, and toss to coat. Cover and chill 2 to 24 hours.

3. Toss in tomatoes, parsley, and remaining ½ cup vinaigrette just before serving. Sprinkle with feta cheese.

*Penne pasta may be substituted.

QUICK TIP You can find most of the ingredients for this recipe in the deli section or olive bar at your local market.

easy side

Fruit Salad:
Toss together fresh fruit, such as raspberries, grapes, blueberries, cantaloupe, strawberries, and melon. Sprinkle with a little sugar and a splash of orange liqueur, if desired.

make ahead

This recipe can be made up to 1 day ahead. Serve cold sprinkled with feta cheese.

Green Bean Pasta Salad with Lemon-Thyme Vinaigrette

MAKES 4 TO 6 SERVINGS   **HANDS-ON TIME** 15 MIN.   **TOTAL TIME** 30 MIN.

Casarecce [cah-sah-RECH-ee] pasta looks similar to a scroll with the long sides curled inward toward the center.

- 12 oz. uncooked casarecce pasta*
- ½ lb. haricots verts (tiny green beans), cut in half lengthwise
- 1 Tbsp. fresh thyme
- 5 tsp. lemon zest, divided
- ¼ cup finely chopped roasted, salted pistachios
- 2 Tbsp. Champagne vinegar
- 1 Tbsp. minced shallots
- 1 garlic clove, minced
- 1 tsp. table salt
- ½ tsp. freshly ground black pepper
- 5 Tbsp. olive oil
- 1½ cups loosely packed arugula

  Toppings: roasted, salted pistachios; freshly grated Parmesan cheese

1. Cook pasta according to package directions, adding green beans to boiling water during last 2 minutes of cooking time; drain. Rinse pasta mixture with cold running water; drain well.

2. Place pasta mixture, thyme, and 3 tsp. lemon zest in a large bowl; toss gently to combine.

3. Whisk together pistachios, next 5 ingredients, and remaining 2 tsp. lemon zest in a small bowl. Add oil in a slow, steady stream, whisking constantly until blended. Drizzle over pasta mixture. Add arugula, and toss gently to coat. Serve with desired toppings.

*Penne pasta may be substituted.

QUICK TIP Don't forget to slice the green beans lengthwise; they will be more tender and absorb the flavors more easily.

make ahead

Prepare this recipe as directed without arugula or toppings; cover and chill until ready to serve. Just before serving, toss in arugula and add desired toppings.

By using fresh pizza dough, piecrust dough, or puff pastry, you can let the store do the work for you so dinner's on the table in a snap.

HARVEST PIZZA, PAGE 50 ▶

Herbed Tomato Tart

MAKES 6 SERVINGS   **HANDS-ON TIME** 25 MIN.   **TOTAL TIME** 1 HOUR, 10 MIN.

We used basil, dill, thyme, and parsley, but just about any combination of herbs that pairs well with tomatoes, such as oregano and tarragon, would work great.

- 2   medium tomatoes, thinly sliced (about ¾ lb.)
- ½   pt. assorted small tomatoes, halved
- ¾   tsp. table salt, divided
- 1   (17.3-oz.) package frozen puff pastry sheets, thawed
- 1   (8-oz.) package shredded mozzarella cheese
- 1   (4-oz.) package crumbled feta cheese
- ¼   cup finely chopped chives
- 1   garlic clove, minced
- ¼   cup finely chopped assorted fresh herbs
- 1   Tbsp. olive oil

1. Preheat oven to 400°. Place tomatoes in a single layer on paper towels; sprinkle with ½ tsp. salt. Let stand 30 minutes. Pat dry with paper towels.

2. Meanwhile, roll 1 pastry sheet into a 14-inch square on a lightly floured surface; place on an ungreased baking sheet. Cut 4 (12- x 1-inch) strips from remaining pastry sheet, and place strips along outer edges of pastry square, forming a border. Reserve remaining pastry for another use.

3. Bake at 400° for 14 minutes or until browned.

4. Sprinkle pastry with mozzarella cheese and next 3 ingredients. Top with tomatoes in a single layer. Sprinkle tomatoes with herbs and remaining ¼ tsp. salt; drizzle with oil.

5. Bake at 400° for 14 to 15 minutes or until cheese melts. Serve immediately.

QUICK TIP Use different varieties of heirloom tomatoes for an extra pop of flavor and color.

easy side

Sautéed Zucchini Spears: Cut 3 medium zucchini in half lengthwise; cut each half crosswise into 2 pieces. Cut each piece into 3 spears. Heat 1½ tsp. olive oil in a large nonstick skillet over medium-high heat; add zucchini and ½ cup coarsely chopped onion. Sauté 5 to 6 minutes or until vegetables are lightly browned. Sprinkle with salt and pepper to taste; toss well.

Breakfast Pizza

MAKES 8 SERVINGS   **HANDS-ON TIME** 15 MIN.   **TOTAL TIME** 50 MIN.

- 1 (8-oz.) can refrigerated crescent rolls
- 1 lb. hot ground pork sausage
- 1 (28-oz.) package frozen hash browns with onions and peppers
- 1 cup (4 oz.) shredded Cheddar cheese
- 4 large eggs
- ½ cup milk
- 1 tsp. table salt
- ½ tsp. freshly ground black pepper

1. Preheat oven to 375°. Unroll crescent roll dough, and press on bottom and partially up sides of a 13- x 9-inch baking dish; press perforations to seal. Bake for 5 minutes.

2. Reduce oven temperature to 350°. Cook sausage in a large skillet over medium-high heat, stirring until sausage crumbles and is no longer pink. Drain well, and sprinkle evenly over crust.

3. Prepare frozen hash browns according to package directions, and spoon evenly over sausage. Sprinkle shredded cheese evenly over hash browns.

4. Whisk together eggs and next 3 ingredients; pour evenly over cheese.

5. Bake at 350° for 30 to 35 minutes or until set.

QUICK TIP You can also bake this in a 12-inch deep-dish pizza pan or cake pan.

easy side

Avocado-and-Papaya Salad: Whisk together 3 Tbsp. fresh lime juice (about 2 limes), 1 Tbsp. honey, and ¼ tsp. table salt in a bowl until well blended. Add 1 medium papaya, peeled and diced, and 2 avocados, peeled and diced; toss gently to coat.

make ahead

Prepare recipe as directed through Step 3. Cover and chill up to 24 hours. Uncover and continue with recipe as directed.

Portobello Pizza

MAKES 6 SERVINGS   **HANDS-ON TIME** 15 MIN.   **TOTAL TIME** 38 MIN.

- 2 large portobello mushroom caps, sliced*
- ½ large onion, sliced
- ½ tsp. table salt
- ½ tsp. black pepper
- Vegetable cooking spray
- 1 Tbsp. balsamic vinegar
- 2 Tbsp. plain yellow cornmeal
- 1 (10-oz.) refrigerated pizza crust dough
- 2 Tbsp. basil pesto
- 2 Tbsp. plain nonfat yogurt
- ¼ cup chopped fresh basil
- 6 fresh mozzarella cheese slices (6 oz.)**
- 5 plum tomatoes, chopped
- 2 Tbsp. shredded Parmesan cheese

1. Preheat oven to 425°. Sauté first 4 ingredients in a large skillet coated with cooking spray over medium-high heat 5 minutes or until onion is tender. Add balsamic vinegar; cook 2 minutes or until liquid is evaporated. Set aside.

2. Sprinkle cornmeal over baking pan; spread out pizza dough. Bake on bottom oven rack at 425° for 5 minutes.

3. Stir together pesto and yogurt. Spread over pizza crust, leaving a 1-inch border. Sprinkle with mushroom mixture and fresh basil. Top with mozzarella cheese and tomatoes. Sprinkle with Parmesan cheese.

4. Bake at 425° on bottom oven rack for 18 minutes or until edges are golden brown and cheese is melted.

*1 (8-oz.) package sliced button mushrooms may be substituted.

**1½ cups (6 oz.) shredded part-skim mozzarella cheese may be substituted.

QUICK TIP Baking the crust on the bottom rack will give you a crisp and crunchy crust.

easy side

▶ **Carrot Slaw:** Combine 4 tsp. rice wine vinegar; 2 tsp. grated fresh ginger; 2 tsp. olive oil; ½ tsp. table salt; ½ tsp. freshly ground pepper; and 4 garlic cloves, minced, in a medium bowl. Add 2 cups matchstick carrots, ½ cup shredded radishes, and 2 Tbsp. chopped fresh cilantro; toss to coat.

QUICK TIP You can use canned pineapple chunks; drain well and blot away extra moisture before topping the pizza.

easy side

Peppery Bacon Green Beans: Cook 6 bacon slices, cut into 1-inch pieces, and ½ medium onion, chopped, in a Dutch oven over medium heat, stirring often, 6 to 8 minutes or until browned. Transfer to a plate, reserving drippings in Dutch oven. Cook 2 (16-oz.) packages frozen green beans in drippings, stirring often, 8 to 10 minutes or until tender. Stir in 2 Tbsp. red wine vinegar, 2 Tbsp. sugar, and bacon mixture. Cook, stirring often, 3 minutes or until thoroughly heated. Season with salt and pepper to taste.

Hawaiian Pizza

MAKES 4 SERVINGS   **HANDS-ON TIME** 10 MIN.   **TOTAL TIME** 50 MIN.

- ¾ cup marinara sauce
- 2 (7-oz.) packages individual prebaked pizza crusts
- 1 cup diced smoked ham
- 1 cup chopped fresh pineapple
- ¼ cup diced green bell pepper
- ½ cup shredded part-skim mozzarella cheese

Preheat oven to 450°. Spread 3 Tbsp. marinara sauce over each of 4 individual pizza crusts. Top each with ¼ cup ham, ¼ cup chopped pineapple, and 1 Tbsp. diced bell pepper. Sprinkle each with 2 Tbsp. cheese. Bake on middle oven rack 10 to 12 minutes.

Note: We tested with Natural Gourmet Kabuli Pizza Crust.

Shrimp Pizza

MAKES 4 SERVINGS   **HANDS-ON TIME** 8 MIN.   **TOTAL TIME** 28 MIN.

Try a new spin on pizza night with pesto, shrimp, and roasted red peppers.

- 1 **(16-oz.) prebaked Italian pizza crust**
- ⅓ **cup refrigerated light pesto or Alfredo sauce**
- 10 **to 12 cooked and peeled large shrimp**
- ½ **cup coarsely chopped jarred roasted red bell peppers**
- ⅓ **cup freshly grated Parmesan cheese**
- 1 **cup loosely packed arugula**
- **Shaved Parmesan cheese**
- **Freshly ground black pepper**

1. Preheat oven to 450°. Spread pizza crust with light pesto or Alfredo sauce. Top with shrimp, red bell peppers, and grated Parmesan cheese.

2. Bake at 450° for 20 minutes or until thoroughly heated. Top with arugula, shaved Parmesan cheese, and freshly ground black pepper.

> **QUICK TIP** Look for cooked and peeled shrimp in the seafood section of your local market.

easy side

Roasted Vegetables:
Preheat oven to 450°. Peel 3 medium-size sweet potatoes (about 1 ½ lb.), and cut into ½-inch cubes. Cut 1 yellow bell pepper into 1-inch pieces. Combine sweet potatoes; bell pepper; 1 medium-size onion, coarsely chopped; 2 Tbsp. olive oil; 1 tsp. table salt; 1 tsp. ground cinnamon; and ¼ tsp. pepper in a large bowl. Place vegetables in a single layer in a lightly greased 15- x 10-inch jelly-roll pan. Bake for 30 to 35 minutes or until sweet potatoes are tender.

Harvest Pizza

MAKES 4 SERVINGS   **HANDS-ON TIME** 10 MIN.   **TOTAL TIME** 28 MIN.

1 lb. pizza dough, at room temperature

Plain yellow cornmeal

1 cup mashed sweet potatoes or leftover sweet potato casserole (without toppings)

1 cup shredded roasted turkey

1 cup shredded spinach

½ cup sliced shiitake mushrooms

½ cup sliced red onion

1½ cups (6 oz.) shredded Havarti cheese

1 tsp. freshly ground Italian seasoning

1. Preheat oven to 450°. Roll pizza crust dough into a 12-inch circle. Transfer to a baking sheet sprinkled with cornmeal. Spread mashed sweet potatoes over dough.

2. Top with turkey, spinach, mushrooms, onion, cheese, and Italian seasoning.

3. Bake at 450° directly on oven rack for 18 minutes or until edges are browned.

Note: We tested with McCormick Italian Herb Seasoning Grinder.

QUICK TIP Havarti cheese is a mild cow's milk cheese that is perfect for melting over this seasonal pizza.

easy side

Broccoli Slaw: Whisk together ¼ cup light sweet Vidalia onion bottled dressing and 2 tsp. cider vinegar in a large bowl. Add 3 cups fresh broccoli slaw, 1 cup chopped Gala apple, and ¼ cup dried cranberries; toss well to coat.

Farmers' Market Pizza

MAKES 6 SERVINGS   **HANDS-ON TIME** 20 MIN.
TOTAL TIME 1 HOUR, 40 MIN., INCLUDING ROASTED VEGETABLES

Plain white cornmeal

1   lb. pizza dough, at room temperature

½   to ¾ cup marinara sauce

1   (8-oz.) package sliced fresh mozzarella cheese

¼   lb. mild Italian sausage, cooked and crumbled

1½   cups Roasted Vegetables

1. Preheat oven to 500°. Lightly dust a baking sheet with cornmeal. Stretch pizza dough into a 12- to 14-inch circle on baking sheet. Spread marinara sauce over dough. Top with mozzarella slices and Italian sausage. Arrange Roasted Vegetables over pizza.

2. Bake at 500° for 15 minutes or until crust is thoroughly cooked, edges are golden, and cheese is melted.

Roasted Vegetables

MAKES 3 CUPS   **HANDS-ON TIME** 10 MIN.   **TOTAL TIME** 55 MIN.

1   medium eggplant, cut into 1-inch pieces

2   large red bell peppers, cut into 1-inch pieces

1   fennel bulb, cut into ¼-inch slices

3   garlic cloves, thinly sliced

3   Tbsp. extra virgin olive oil

1   tsp. kosher salt

½   tsp. freshly ground black pepper

2   Tbsp. chopped fresh basil

1   Tbsp. white balsamic vinegar

Preheat oven to 450°. Toss together first 7 ingredients in a bowl until coated. Spread vegetables in a single layer in a 15- x 10-inch jelly-roll pan; bake for 45 to 50 minutes or until vegetables are tender and slightly charred, stirring halfway through. Toss with basil and vinegar.

QUICK TIP For maximum flavor and nutritional value, use fresh vegetables within one or two days after purchasing them.

easy side

▶ **Cucumber-and-Grape Tomato Salad:** Whisk together ⅓ cup white balsamic vinegar and ¼ cup pepper jelly. Toss with 1 quartered and thinly sliced English cucumber, 1 quartered and thinly sliced small red onion, 4 cups loosely packed fresh arugula, 2 cups halved grape tomatoes, and 1 cup sliced yellow bell pepper.

Muffuletta Calzones

MAKES 4 SERVINGS   **HANDS-ON TIME** 20 MIN.   **TOTAL TIME** 40 MIN.

Pizza dough from the grocery store bakery wraps up traditional muffuletta ingredients—salami, ham, cheese, and olives.

- 1 cup jarred mixed pickled vegetables, rinsed and finely chopped
- 1 (7-oz.) package shredded provolone-Italian cheese blend
- 8 thin slices Genoa salami, chopped (about ⅛ lb.)
- ½ cup diced cooked ham
- ¼ cup sliced pimiento-stuffed Spanish olives
- 2 Tbsp. olive oil, divided
- 1 lb. pizza dough, at room temperature
- 2 Tbsp. grated Parmesan cheese

1. Preheat oven to 425°. Stir together pickled vegetables, next 4 ingredients, and 1 Tbsp. olive oil.

2. Place dough on a lightly floured surface. Cut dough into 4 equal pieces. Roll each piece into a 7-inch circle. Place 2 dough circles on a lightly greased baking sheet. Spoon vegetable mixture on top of dough circles, mounding mixture on dough and leaving a 1-inch border. Moisten edges of dough with water, and top with remaining 2 dough circles. Press and crimp edges to seal.

3. Cut small slits in tops of dough circles to allow steam to escape. Brush with remaining 1 Tbsp. olive oil, and sprinkle with Parmesan cheese.

4. Bake at 425° for 20 to 24 minutes or until golden brown. Cut in half to serve.

QUICK TIP Seal and crimp edges of calzones well, so they don't open up during baking.

easy side

Broccoli with Garlic: Microwave 1 (12-oz.) package fresh broccoli florets; 1 garlic clove, minced; 2 Tbsp. water; and ½ tsp. table salt in a microwave-safe glass bowl, covered with plastic wrap, at HIGH 3 to 4 minutes or until tender.

make ahead

Prepare recipe as directed through Step 3. Freeze unbaked calzones, in zip-top plastic bags. Thaw calzones 30 minutes before baking as directed.

Savory Hand Pies

MAKES 18 PIES   **HANDS-ON TIME** 20 MIN.   **TOTAL TIME** 48 MIN.

These pies are the perfect after-school snack or meal on the go.

- 1   cup finely chopped roasted turkey
- ¾   cup mashed potatoes
- ½   (8-oz.) package cream cheese, softened
- ½   cup cut green beans, cooked
- 1   carrot, grated
- 2   Tbsp. chopped fresh parsley
- 1½   (14.1-oz.) packages refrigerated piecrusts
- 1   large egg, beaten
-   Poppy seeds (optional)
-   Turkey gravy, warmed

1. Stir together first 6 ingredients. Add salt and pepper to taste.

2. Preheat oven to 400°. Unroll each piecrust. Lightly roll each into a 12-inch circle. Cut each piecrust into 6 circles using a 4-inch round cutter. Place about 3 Tbsp. turkey mixture just below center of each dough circle. Fold dough over filling, pressing and folding edges to seal.

3. Arrange pies on a lightly greased baking sheet. Brush with egg, and, if desired, sprinkle with poppy seeds.

4. Bake at 400° for 18 to 20 minutes or until golden brown. Serve with warm gravy.

QUICK TIP Use your leftover turkey, mashed potatoes, and green beans to bake up these little pies.

easy side

Parmesan Mashed Potatoes: Prepare 1 (24-oz.) package refrigerated mashed potatoes according to package directions. Stir in ¼ cup freshly grated Parmesan cheese, 2 Tbsp. chopped fresh chives, and ½ tsp. freshly ground pepper.

make ahead

Unbaked pies can be frozen up to 1 month. Bake frozen pies at 400° for 30 to 32 minutes or until golden brown.

Seafood Pot Pie

MAKES 6 SERVINGS   **HANDS-ON TIME** 15 MIN.
TOTAL TIME 3 HOURS, 15 MIN.

- ¼ cup butter
- 1 cup chopped onion or 1 leek, thinly sliced
- 2 tsp. jarred minced garlic
- 1 (8-oz.) package sliced baby portobello mushrooms
- ¼ cup all-purpose flour
- 1 cup half-and-half
- 1 cup chicken broth
- 1 (11-oz.) package frozen baby broccoli blend
- 1 (1-lb.) cod fillet, cut into 2-inch pieces
- ½ lb. fresh lump crabmeat, drained and picked free of shell
- ½ tsp. table salt
- ½ tsp. freshly ground black pepper
- ½ (17.3-oz.) package frozen puff pastry sheets, thawed
  Parchment paper
- 1 egg yolk, beaten
- ¼ cup dry sherry

1. Melt butter in a large skillet over medium-high heat. Add onion, garlic, and mushrooms; sauté 5 minutes. Whisk in flour until smooth. Cook 1 minute, whisking constantly. Gradually whisk in half-and-half and broth; cook over medium heat, whisking constantly, until thickened and bubbly. Transfer to a 3½-qt. slow cooker. Stir in vegetables. Cover and cook on LOW 2 hours.

2. Uncover and stir in cod, crabmeat, salt, and pepper. (Cooker will be almost full.) Cover and cook on HIGH 1 hour or until fish flakes with a fork.

3. Preheat oven to 400°. Roll out 1 pastry sheet on a lightly floured surface until smooth. Using a paring knife, cut out pastry to an oval about the size of the top of your slow cooker. Place pastry on a parchment paper-lined baking sheet. Brush with egg yolk. Bake for 14 to 15 minutes. Stir sherry into pot pie in slow cooker. Top pot pie with pastry lid just before serving. Serve immediately.

QUICK TIP Use parchment paper to trace top of slow cooker and use this template to cut puff pastry to the perfect size.

easy side

Mixed Greens with Garlic Oil Dressing:
Whisk together 2 garlic cloves, minced; 2 tsp. chopped fresh oregano; ½ tsp. freshly ground pepper; ¼ tsp. table salt; 3 Tbsp. fresh lime juice; and 2 Tbsp. water in a large bowl. Whisk in 3 Tbsp. olive oil. Add 2 (5-oz.) packages spring greens mix, and toss gently to coat.

Italian-Style Pizza Pot Pie

MAKES 4 TO 6 SERVINGS **HANDS-ON TIME** 15 MIN. **TOTAL TIME** 1 HOUR, 15 MIN.

- ¾ lb. ground round
- ¼ lb. mild Italian sausage, casings removed
- 1 small onion, chopped
- 2 garlic cloves, minced
- 1 (8-oz.) package sliced fresh mushrooms
- 1 (26-oz.) jar tomato-and-basil pasta sauce
- ½ tsp. dried Italian seasoning
- ¼ tsp. table salt
- 1 (13.8-oz.) package refrigerated pizza crust dough
- Parchment paper
- 1 cup (4 oz.) shredded Italian five-cheese blend

1. Preheat oven to 450°. Cook ground round and sausage in a large skillet over medium-high heat, stirring often, 8 to 10 minutes or until meat crumbles and is no longer pink. Drain beef mixture, reserving 1 tsp. drippings in skillet. Reduce heat to medium.

2. Sauté onion in hot drippings 2 minutes. Add garlic, and cook 1 minute or until tender. Add mushrooms, and sauté 8 to 10 minutes or until most of liquid has evaporated. Stir in beef mixture, pasta sauce, Italian seasoning, and salt. Bring to a light boil, and simmer 5 minutes.

3. Meanwhile, unroll dough on a lightly floured piece of parchment paper. Invert 1 (9-inch) round baking dish or pie plate onto center of dough. Cut dough around edge of baking dish, making a 9-inch circle. Remove excess dough around baking dish; cover and chill, reserving for another use. Remove baking dish.

4. Pour beef mixture into baking dish, and sprinkle with cheese. Immediately top with dough circle. Cut an "X" in top of dough for steam to escape. Place baking dish on an aluminum foil-lined baking sheet.

5. Bake at 450° for 16 to 20 minutes or until crust is golden brown. Let stand 10 minutes before serving.

QUICK TIP If you want more heat in this casserole, you can substitute spicy Italian sausage.

easy side

Greek Salad: Combine 2½ cups mixed salad greens, ½ cup sliced cucumber, ½ cup sliced red onion, 3 Tbsp. crumbled feta cheese, 1 Tbsp. fresh lemon juice, 1 Tbsp. extra virgin olive oil, ¼ tsp. dried oregano, and ⅛ tsp. dried crushed red pepper in a large bowl, tossing well to coat.

1 PASTA

2 PASTRY & PIZZA DOUGH

3 EGGS

4 SALAD GREENS

5 ROTISSERIE CHICKEN

6 CHICKEN BREASTS

7 PORK LOIN & CHOPS

8 GROUND MEAT

Eggs are so versatile and easy to keep at the ready for a satisfying meal any time of the day.

ROASTED SWEET POTATO-AND-ONION TART, PAGE 85 ▶

Fried Egg Sandwiches

MAKES 4 SERVINGS   **HANDS-ON TIME** 25 MIN.   **TOTAL TIME** 27 MIN.

- 4 (½-inch-thick) challah bread slices
- 2 Tbsp. butter, melted
- 1 (0.9-oz.) envelope hollandaise sauce mix
- ¼ tsp. lemon zest
- 1½ tsp. fresh lemon juice, divided
- 2 cups loosely packed arugula
- ½ cup loosely packed fresh flat-leaf parsley leaves
- ¼ cup thinly sliced red onion
- 3 tsp. extra virgin olive oil, divided
- 4 large eggs
- ¼ tsp. kosher salt
- ¼ tsp. freshly ground black pepper
- 12 thin pancetta slices, cooked
- 2 Tbsp. chopped sun-dried tomatoes

1. Preheat broiler with oven rack 5 to 6 inches from heat. Brush both sides of bread with butter; place on an aluminum foil-lined broiler pan. Broil 1 to 2 minutes on each side or until lightly toasted.

2. Prepare hollandaise sauce according to package directions; stir in zest and ½ tsp. lemon juice. Keep warm.

3. Toss together arugula, next 2 ingredients, 2 tsp. olive oil, and remaining 1 tsp. lemon juice.

4. Heat remaining 1 tsp. olive oil in a large nonstick skillet over medium heat. Gently break eggs into hot skillet; sprinkle with salt and pepper. Cook 2 to 3 minutes on each side or to desired degree of doneness.

5. Top bread slices with arugula mixture, pancetta slices, and fried eggs. Spoon hollandaise sauce over each egg, and sprinkle with tomatoes. Serve immediately.

QUICK TIP Crispy cooked bacon is a great substitute for pancetta, if you like.

easy side

Balsamic Berries: Combine 1 cup quartered small strawberries, 1 cup blueberries, 1 cup raspberries, and 1 Tbsp. balsamic glaze in a bowl; let stand 5 minutes. Spoon berry mixture into small bowls. Top with sour cream.

Scrambled Egg Muffin Sliders

MAKES 12 SERVINGS **HANDS-ON TIME** 22 MIN. **TOTAL TIME** 52 MIN.

- 2 cups self-rising white cornmeal mix
- 1 Tbsp. sugar
- 1½ cups buttermilk
- 1 large egg
- 4 Tbsp. butter, melted
- 1 cup (4 oz.) shredded sharp Cheddar cheese
- 6 bacon slices, cooked and crumbled
- Vegetable cooking spray
- 8 large eggs
- ½ tsp. Creole seasoning
- 1 Tbsp. butter

1. Preheat oven to 425°. Heat a 12-cup muffin pan in oven 5 minutes. Combine cornmeal mix and sugar in a medium bowl; make a well in center of mixture. Stir together buttermilk and egg; add to cornmeal mixture, stirring just until dry ingredients are moistened. Stir in melted butter, cheese, and bacon. Remove pan from oven, and coat with cooking spray. Spoon batter into hot muffin pan, filling almost completely full.

2. Bake at 425° for 15 to 20 minutes or until golden. Remove from pan to a wire rack, and let cool 10 minutes.

3. Whisk together eggs, 1 Tbsp. water, and Creole seasoning in a medium bowl. Melt 1 Tbsp. butter in a large nonstick skillet. Add egg mixture, and cook, without stirring, 2 to 3 minutes or until eggs begin to set on bottom. Gently draw cooked edges away from sides of pan to form large pieces. Cook, stirring occasionally, 4 to 5 minutes or until eggs are thickened and moist. (Do not overstir.)

4. Cut muffins in half, and spoon eggs over bottom halves. Cover with top halves of muffins.

QUICK TIP The trick is heating the pan beforehand, which will result in a nice crispy bottom on the muffin.

make ahead

Bake muffins ahead. Warm muffins just before cooking egg mixture; assemble and serve.

Spicy Ham-and-Eggs Benedict

MAKES 4 SERVINGS   **HANDS-ON TIME** 15 MIN.   **TOTAL TIME** 1 HOUR, 5 MIN.

- 4 frozen biscuits
- 2 Tbsp. butter, melted
- 3 Tbsp. chopped fresh chives, divided
- 1 (0.9-oz.) envelope hollandaise sauce mix
- 1 cup milk
- 1 Tbsp. lemon juice
- ¾ cup chopped lean ham
- ¼ to ½ tsp. ground red pepper
- ½ tsp. white vinegar
- 4 large eggs
- 2 cups loosely packed arugula
- 1 small avocado, sliced

1. Bake biscuits according to package directions. Preheat oven to 375°. Combine melted butter and 1 Tbsp. chives; split biscuits, and brush with butter mixture. Place biscuits, buttered sides up, on a baking sheet, and bake for 5 minutes or until toasted.

2. Cook hollandaise sauce mix according to package directions, using 1 cup milk and 1 Tbsp. lemon juice and omitting butter. Cook ham, stirring occasionally, in a medium-size nonstick skillet over medium heat 3 to 4 minutes or until browned. Stir ham and ground red pepper into hollandaise sauce; keep warm.

3. Add water to a depth of 2 inches in a large saucepan. Bring to a boil; reduce heat, and maintain at a light simmer. Add white vinegar. Break eggs, and slip into water, 1 at a time, as close as possible to surface of water. Simmer 3 to 5 minutes or to desired degree of doneness. Remove with a slotted spoon.

4. Place bottom biscuit halves, buttered sides up, on each of 4 individual serving plates. Top evenly with arugula, avocado, and poached eggs. Spoon hollandaise sauce evenly on top of each egg. Sprinkle with remaining 2 Tbsp. chives, and add pepper to taste. Top with remaining biscuit halves, and serve immediately.

QUICK TIP Poached eggs sound tricky, but are actually very quick and simple. Practice makes perfect!

easy side

Watermelon Cooler: Process 4 cups seeded watermelon cubes, ⅓ cup apple juice, 2 Tbsp. fresh lime juice, 1 tsp. chopped fresh mint, ¼ to ½ tsp. ground ginger, and, if desired, 1 Tbsp. honey in a blender or food processor until smooth, stopping to scrape down sides. Cover and chill 1 hour. Garnish with lime wedges and fresh mint sprigs.

QUICK TIP Peeling eggs under running water helps the shell detach easily without harming the egg.

make ahead

Make Parmesan Vinaigrette up to a week ahead; keep covered and refrigerated.

Farmer Salad

MAKES 8 SERVINGS   **HANDS-ON TIME** 25 MIN.
TOTAL TIME 45 MIN., INCLUDING PARMESAN VINAIGRETTE

- 8   large eggs
- 8   thick bacon slices, cooked and crumbled
- 8   cups loosely packed baby arugula
- 4   cups trimmed frisée
- 2   cups thinly sliced radicchio
- 2   cups brioche or challah bread cubes, toasted
- ½   cup shaved Parmesan cheese
- Parmesan Vinaigrette

1. Bring 12 cups water to a boil in a large Dutch oven. Add eggs; boil 5 (soft cooked) to 7 (hard cooked) minutes. Remove from heat, and let eggs stand in hot water 1 minute; drain. Peel under cold running water. Cut eggs in half.

2. Toss together bacon and next 5 ingredients. Divide mixture among 8 bowls. Top each with 2 egg halves. Serve with Parmesan Vinaigrette.

Parmesan Vinaigrette

MAKES 1½ CUPS   **HANDS-ON TIME** 8 MIN.   **TOTAL TIME** 8 MIN.

- 1¼   cups freshly grated Parmesan cheese
- ½   cup red wine vinegar
- 4   anchovy fillets
- 1   tsp. lemon zest
- 1   Tbsp. fresh lemon juice
- 1   garlic clove, pressed
- 1   tsp. Dijon mustard
- 1   tsp. Worcestershire sauce
- ½   cup olive oil

Process first 8 ingredients in a blender or food processor until smooth. Add olive oil in a slow, steady stream, processing until smooth. Season with salt and pepper to taste.

Sautéed Greens with Olive Oil-Fried Eggs

MAKES 2 SERVINGS   **HANDS-ON TIME** 20 MIN.   **TOTAL TIME** 30 MIN.

- 2 **cups butternut squash cubes (1 small squash)**
- 1¼ **cups olive oil, divided**
- 1 **tsp. kosher salt, divided**
- 1 **medium-size onion, halved and thinly sliced**
- 2 **(5-oz.) packages mixed baby braising greens**
- ¼ **cup blanched hazelnuts, toasted and chopped**
- 2 **Tbsp. dry sherry**
- 2 **large eggs**
- ¼ **cup crumbled goat cheese**

1. Preheat oven to 450°. Toss squash with 2 Tbsp. olive oil, and spread in a single layer on a baking sheet; sprinkle with ½ tsp. salt. Bake for 20 minutes or until squash is soft and golden brown, stirring occasionally.

2. Meanwhile, sauté onion in 2 Tbsp. hot oil in a large skillet over medium heat 10 minutes or until onion is tender. Add greens, next 2 ingredients, and squash, tossing to coat. Sprinkle with remaining ½ tsp. salt. Cook, stirring often, 2 minutes or just until greens begin to wilt.

3. Pour remaining 1 cup olive oil to depth of ⅓ inch into a small non-stick skillet. Heat oil over medium-high just until it begins to smoke. Reduce heat to medium. Break 1 egg into a ramekin or small bowl. Holding dish as close to surface as possible, carefully slip egg into oil. Spoon oil over egg for about 30 seconds or until white is cooked and crispy on edges. Remove egg from oil using a slotted spoon, dabbing with paper towels to absorb oil; transfer egg to a plate. Repeat with remaining egg.

4. Sprinkle greens with goat cheese. Top with fried eggs. Season with salt and pepper to taste.

QUICK TIP The key to perfectly fried eggs is frying them fast and basting the yolks with the hot oil until they are opaque.

easy side

Cornbread Waffles: Prepare batter from 2 (6-oz.) packages buttermilk cornbread mix according to package directions. Cook batter, in batches, in a preheated, oiled waffle iron until done.

QUICK TIP Using paper towel to blot chopped tomato allows scrambled eggs to get great tomato flavor without being watery.

easy side

Creamy Grits: Bring 2 (14-oz.) cans chicken broth and 2 cups milk to a boil in a saucepan over medium-high heat; reduce heat to low, and whisk in 1 cup uncooked regular grits. Cook, whisking occasionally, 15 to 20 minutes or until thickened and creamy.

Farmers' Market Scramble

MAKES 12 SERVINGS   **HANDS-ON TIME** 10 MIN.   **TOTAL TIME** 24 MIN.

Hearty scrambled eggs get a punch of flavor with fresh herbs and tomato.

24	large eggs
½	cup milk
¼	cup whipping cream
1 ½	tsp. table salt
½	tsp. freshly ground black pepper
½	tsp. hot sauce
¼	cup butter, divided
1	large tomato, chopped and drained on a paper towel
⅓	cup chopped fresh chives
¼	cup chopped fresh flat-leaf parsley

1. Whisk together first 6 ingredients in a large bowl.

2. Melt 2 Tbsp. butter in a large nonstick skillet over medium heat; add half of egg mixture, and cook, without stirring, until eggs begin to set on bottom. Draw a spatula across bottom of skillet to form large curds. Cook until eggs are thickened but still moist. (Do not stir constantly.) Stir in half of tomato. Remove from heat, and transfer to a warm platter. Repeat procedure with remaining butter, egg mixture, and tomato.

3. Sprinkle whole platter of eggs with chives and parsley; serve hot.

Spinach-and-Cheese Omelet

MAKES 1 SERVING   **HANDS-ON TIME** 14 MIN.   **TOTAL TIME** 14 MIN.

- 2 large eggs
- 1 Tbsp. butter
- 1 cup coarsely chopped spinach
- ⅓ cup chopped tomatoes
- ⅛ tsp. table salt
- ⅓ cup (1 ½ oz.) shredded Swiss cheese
- ⅛ tsp. black pepper

1. Process eggs and 2 Tbsp. water in a blender until blended. Melt butter in an 8-inch nonstick skillet over medium heat; add spinach and tomatoes, and sauté 1 minute or until spinach is wilted. Add salt and egg mixture to skillet.

2. As egg mixture starts to cook, gently lift edges of omelet with a spatula, and tilt pan so uncooked egg mixture flows underneath, cooking until almost set (about 1 minute). Cover skillet, and cook 1 minute.

3. Sprinkle omelet with cheese and pepper. Fold omelet in half, allowing cheese to melt. Slide cooked omelet onto a serving plate, and add salt to taste.

> **QUICK TIP** Use a shallow pan with gently curved sides, a flat bottom, and a long handle for the best omelet.

easy side

Corn Muffins:
Preheat oven to 400°. Lightly grease a 24-cup miniature muffin pan. Stir together 1 (6.5-oz.) package corn muffin mix, ⅓ cup fat-free milk, 2 Tbsp. canola oil, 2 egg whites, and 1 cup frozen white shoepeg corn in a medium bowl just until blended. Spoon batter into prepared muffin pan. Bake 11 minutes. Spray tops of muffins with cooking spray; bake 2 more minutes. Remove from oven; cool in pan 2 minutes.

Sunny Skillet Breakfast

MAKES 6 SERVINGS   **HANDS-ON TIME** 15 MIN.   **TOTAL TIME** 50 MIN.

- 3 (8-oz.) baking potatoes, peeled and shredded (about 3 cups firmly packed)*
- 1 Tbsp. butter
- 2 Tbsp. vegetable oil
- 1 small red bell pepper, diced
- 1 medium onion, diced
- 1 garlic clove, pressed
- ¾ tsp. table salt, divided
- 6 large eggs
- ¼ tsp. black pepper

1. Preheat oven to 350°. Place shredded potatoes in a large bowl; add cold water to cover. Let stand 5 minutes; drain and pat dry.

2. Melt butter with oil in a 10-inch cast-iron skillet over medium heat. Add bell pepper and onion, and sauté 3 to 5 minutes or until tender. Add garlic; sauté 1 minute. Stir in shredded potatoes and ½ tsp. salt; cook, stirring often, 10 minutes or until potatoes are golden and tender.

3. Remove from heat. Make 6 indentations in potato mixture, using back of a spoon. Break 1 egg into each indentation. Sprinkle eggs with pepper and remaining ¼ tsp. salt.

4. Bake at 350° for 12 to 14 minutes or until eggs are set. Serve immediately.

3 cups firmly packed frozen shredded potatoes may be substituted, omitting Step 1.

QUICK TIP Soaking in cold water keeps potatoes from turning gray before cooking. Drain and pat dry with paper towels.

easy side

Grapefruit Salad: Toss 1 (5-oz.) package mixed salad greens with 2 cups refrigerated red grapefruit sections, 2 cups sliced avocado, ½ cup sweetened dried cranberries, and ⅓ cup bottled poppyseed dressing.

Tomato-Herb Mini Frittatas

MAKES 8 SERVINGS　　**HANDS-ON TIME** 15 MIN.　　**TOTAL TIME** 15 MIN.

- 12　large eggs
- 1　cup half-and-half
- ½　tsp. table salt
- ¼　tsp. freshly ground black pepper
- 2　Tbsp. chopped fresh chives
- 1　Tbsp. chopped fresh parsley
- 1　tsp. chopped fresh oregano
- 1　pt. grape tomatoes, halved
- 1½　cups (6 oz.) shredded Italian three-cheese blend

1. Preheat oven to 450°. Process first 4 ingredients in a blender until blended. Stir together chives and next 2 ingredients in a small bowl. Place 8 lightly greased 4-inch (6-oz.) ramekins on 2 baking sheets; layer tomatoes, 1 cup cheese, and chive mixture in ramekins. Pour egg mixture over top, and sprinkle with remaining ½ cup cheese.

2. Bake at 450° for 7 minutes, placing 1 baking sheet on middle oven rack and other on lower oven rack. Switch baking sheets, and bake 7 to 8 more minutes or until set. Remove top baking sheet from oven; transfer bottom sheet to middle rack, and bake 1 to 2 more minutes or until lightly browned.

QUICK TIP Rotating the baking sheets near the end of cooking time allows the tops to brown slightly.

easy side

Garlic Mashed Potatoes: Microwave 1 (24-oz.) package frozen steam-and-mash potatoes according to package directions. Transfer cooked potatoes to a large bowl, and stir in ⅓ cup buttermilk; 2 garlic cloves, finely chopped; ½ tsp. table salt; ½ tsp. black pepper; and 2 Tbsp. butter. Mash to desired consistency.

make ahead

Prepare recipe as directed through Step 2. Cover and refrigerate up to 4 hours. Uncover and continue with recipe as directed.

Caramelized Onion Quiche

MAKES 6 TO 8 SERVINGS   **HANDS-ON TIME** 45 MIN.
TOTAL TIME 2 HOURS

Gruyère cheese and bacon combine with caramelized onions for a quiche that can't be beat.

- 1 (14.1-oz.) package refrigerated piecrusts
- 3 large sweet onions, sliced (about 1 ½ lb.)
- 2 Tbsp. olive oil
- ½ cup chopped fresh flat-leaf parsley
- 6 cooked bacon slices, crumbled
- 2 cups (8 oz.) shredded Gruyère cheese
- 1½ cups half-and-half
- 4 large eggs
- ½ tsp. table salt
- ¼ tsp. freshly ground black pepper
- ¼ tsp. ground nutmeg

1. Preheat oven to 425°. Unroll piecrusts; stack on a lightly greased surface. Roll stacked piecrusts into a 12-inch circle. Fit piecrust into a 10-inch deep-dish tart pan with removable bottom; press into fluted edges. Trim off excess piecrust along edges. Line piecrust with aluminum foil or parchment paper, and fill with pie weights or dried beans. Place pan on a foil-lined baking sheet. Bake for 12 minutes. Remove weights and foil, and bake 8 more minutes. Cool completely on baking sheet on a wire rack (about 15 minutes). Reduce oven temperature to 350°.

2. Meanwhile, cook onions in hot oil in a large skillet over medium-high heat, stirring often, 15 to 20 minutes or until onions are caramel colored. Remove from heat, and stir in parsley and bacon. Place half of onion mixture in tart shell, and top with half of cheese; repeat with remaining onion mixture and cheese.

3. Whisk together half-and-half and next 4 ingredients; pour over cheese.

4. Bake at 350° for 40 to 45 minutes or until set. Cool on baking sheet on a wire rack 15 minutes before serving.

Roasted Sweet Potato-and-Onion Tart

MAKES 6 TO 8 SERVINGS   **HANDS-ON TIME** 30 MIN.   **TOTAL TIME** 2 HOURS, 40 MIN.

- 3 cups ¾-inch-cubed sweet potatoes (about 1½ lb.)
- 1 cup chopped red onion
- 2 Tbsp. olive oil
- 1 tsp. seasoned pepper
- 6 cooked bacon slices, crumbled
- ¼ cup chopped fresh flat-leaf parsley
- 1 (14.1-oz.) package refrigerated piecrusts
- 2 cups (8 oz.) shredded Gruyère cheese
- 1½ cups half-and-half
- 4 large eggs
- 1 tsp. chopped fresh rosemary
- ½ tsp. table salt

Garnish: fresh rosemary sprigs

1. Preheat oven to 425°. Toss together first 4 ingredients in a large bowl; arrange mixture in a single layer in a lightly greased 15- x 10-inch jelly-roll pan. Bake for 20 minutes or just until potatoes are tender, stirring after 10 minutes. Cool completely in pan on a wire rack (about 30 minutes). Stir in bacon and parsley.

2. Unroll piecrusts; stack on a lightly greased surface. Roll stacked piecrusts into a 12-inch circle. Fit piecrust into a 10-inch deep-dish tart pan with removable bottom; press into fluted edges. Trim off excess piecrust along edges. Line piecrust with aluminum foil or parchment paper, and fill with pie weights or dried beans.

3. Bake at 425° for 12 minutes. Remove weights and foil; bake 5 more minutes. Cool completely on baking sheet on a wire rack (about 15 minutes). Reduce oven temperature to 350°.

4. Layer half of sweet potato mixture and half of cheese in tart shell; repeat layers once.

5. Whisk together half-and-half and next 3 ingredients; pour over cheese. Bake at 350° on lowest oven rack 35 to 40 minutes or until set. Cool tart on baking sheet on a wire rack 15 minutes.

QUICK TIP Gruyère is a mild, nutty cheese that is perfect for melting. If you can't find it, Swiss cheese is a good substitute.

easy side

Simple Spinach Salad: Gently toss fresh baby spinach leaves, and thinly sliced red onions with bottled balsamic vinaigrette.

make ahead

Prepare recipe as directed through Step 4. Cover and refrigerate up to 4 hours. Uncover and continue with recipe as directed.

Kentucky Hot Brown Tart

MAKES 6 TO 8 SERVINGS   **HANDS-ON TIME** 20 MIN.   **TOTAL TIME** 1 HOUR, 50 MIN.

QUICK TIP Plum tomatoes are best in this recipe because they are less likely to water out when baked than regular tomatoes.

- 1 (14.1-oz.) package refrigerated piecrusts
- 1½ cups chopped cooked turkey
- 2 cups (8 oz.) shredded white Cheddar cheese
- ¼ cup finely chopped fresh chives
- 6 bacon slices, cooked and crumbled
- 1½ cups half-and-half
- 4 large eggs
- ½ tsp. table salt
- ¼ tsp. freshly ground black pepper
- 2 plum tomatoes, cut into ¼-inch-thick slices
- ½ cup freshly grated Parmesan cheese

1. Preheat oven to 425°. Unroll piecrusts; stack on a lightly greased surface. Roll stacked piecrusts into a 12-inch circle. Fit piecrust into a 10-inch deep-dish tart pan with removable bottom; press into fluted edges. Trim off excess piecrust along edges. Line piecrust with aluminum foil or parchment paper, and fill with pie weights or dried beans. Place pan on a foil-lined baking sheet. Bake for 12 minutes. Remove weights and foil from piecrust, and bake 8 more minutes. Cool completely on baking sheet on a wire rack (about 15 minutes). Reduce oven temperature to 350°.

2. Layer turkey and next 3 ingredients in tart shell on baking sheet. Whisk together half-and-half and next 3 ingredients; pour over turkey.

3. Bake at 350° for 30 to 40 minutes or until set.

4. Place tomatoes in a single layer on paper towels; press tomatoes lightly with paper towels. Arrange over top of tart, and sprinkle with Parmesan cheese. Bake 10 to 15 more minutes or until cheese is melted. Cool on baking sheet on wire rack 15 minutes.

Creamy Egg Strata

MAKES 8 TO 10 SERVINGS　　**HANDS-ON TIME** 35 MIN.　　**TOTAL TIME** 10 HOURS, 10 MIN.

- ½ (16-oz.) French bread loaf, cubed (about 5 cups)
- 6 Tbsp. butter, divided
- 2 cups (8 oz.) shredded Swiss cheese
- ½ cup freshly grated Parmesan cheese
- ⅓ cup chopped onion
- 1 tsp. minced garlic
- 3 Tbsp. all-purpose flour
- 1½ cups chicken broth
- ¾ cup dry white wine
- ½ tsp. table salt
- ½ tsp. freshly ground black pepper
- ¼ tsp. ground nutmeg
- ½ cup sour cream
- 8 large eggs, lightly beaten
- Garnish: chopped fresh chives

1. Place bread cubes in a well-buttered 13- x 9-inch baking dish. Melt 3 Tbsp. butter, and drizzle over bread cubes. Sprinkle with cheeses.

2. Melt remaining 3 Tbsp. butter in a medium saucepan over medium heat; add onion and garlic. Sauté 2 to 3 minutes or until tender. Whisk in flour until smooth; cook, whisking constantly, 2 to 3 minutes or until lightly browned. Whisk in broth and next 4 ingredients until blended. Bring mixture to a boil; reduce heat to medium-low, and simmer, stirring occasionally, 15 minutes or until thickened. Remove from heat. Stir in sour cream. Add salt and pepper to taste.

3. Gradually whisk about one-fourth of hot sour cream mixture into eggs; add egg mixture to remaining sour cream mixture, whisking constantly. Pour mixture over cheese in baking dish. Cover with plastic wrap, and chill 8 to 24 hours.

4. Let strata stand at room temperature 1 hour. Preheat oven to 350°. Remove plastic wrap, and bake for 30 minutes or until set. Serve immediately.

QUICK TIP Letting this casserole sit overnight is crucial for creating a custard-like texture.

make ahead

Prepare recipe as directed through Step 3. Cover and refrigerate up to 24 hours. Uncover and continue with recipe as directed.

Take advantage of the great variety of washed, chopped, and bagged greens that are so widely available, by making any of these vibrant salads, soups, or pastas.

BLT SALAD, PAGE 101 ▶

Three Sisters Salad

MAKES 8 TO 10 SERVINGS   **HANDS-ON TIME** 20 MIN.
TOTAL TIME 3 HOURS, 10 MIN., INCLUDING BALSAMIC VINAIGRETTE

- 2   lb. butternut squash
- 2   Tbsp. olive oil
- 1   (15.5-oz.) can cannellini beans, drained and rinsed
- 2   cups fresh corn kernels
- ½   small red onion, sliced
- ½   cup chopped fresh basil
- Balsamic Vinaigrette
- 3   cups loosely packed arugula

1. Preheat oven to 400°. Peel and seed butternut squash; cut into ¾-inch cubes. Toss squash with olive oil to coat; place in a single layer in a lightly greased aluminum foil-lined 15- x 10-inch jelly-roll pan. Bake for 20 minutes or until squash is just tender and begins to brown (do not overcook), stirring once after 10 minutes. Cool completely (about 20 minutes).

2. Toss together cannellini beans, next 4 ingredients, and squash in a large bowl; cover and chill 2 to 4 hours. Toss with arugula just before serving.

Balsamic Vinaigrette

MAKES ½ CUP   **HANDS-ON TIME** 5 MIN.   **TOTAL TIME** 5 MIN.

- 2   Tbsp. balsamic vinegar
- 1   large shallot, minced
- 1   tsp. minced garlic
- ½   Tbsp. light brown sugar
- ¼   tsp. table salt
- ¼   tsp. seasoned pepper
- ¼   cup canola oil

Whisk together first 6 ingredients. Gradually add canola oil in a slow, steady stream, whisking until blended.

QUICK TIP Look for pre-chopped butternut squash in the produce section to save time and effort.

easy side

Garlic Bread: Preheat oven to 350°. Stir together 3 garlic cloves, minced; 2 Tbsp. extra virgin olive oil; 2 Tbsp. butter, melted; 1 Tbsp. chopped fresh chives; and ½ tsp. dried crushed red pepper in a small bowl. Cut 1 (16-oz.) French bread loaf in half lengthwise. Brush cut sides with garlic mixture; place on a baking sheet. Bake at 350° for 13 to 15 minutes or until golden brown. Cut each bread half into 8 slices.

Blueberry Fields Salad

MAKES 8 SERVINGS   **HANDS-ON TIME** 20 MIN.   **TOTAL TIME** 20 MIN.

Spring greens and baby spinach get a lift with fresh blueberries, red onion, and the tang of blue cheese in this springy salad.

½   cup balsamic vinegar

⅓   cup blueberry preserves

⅓   cup olive oil

2   (5.5-oz.) packages spring greens and baby spinach mix

2   cups fresh blueberries

1   cup chopped walnuts, toasted

1   small red onion, halved and sliced

1   cup crumbled blue cheese

1. Whisk together balsamic vinegar, next 2 ingredients, and salt and pepper to taste in a small bowl.

2. Combine spinach mix and next 4 ingredients in a large bowl. Drizzle with desired amount of vinaigrette, and toss to combine. Serve immediately with remaining vinaigrette.

QUICK TIP By using fruit preserves in the dressing, you're adding big flavor with little effort!

easy side

Grilled Three-Cheese Sandwiches: Stir together ¼ cup softened butter and 1 Tbsp. grated Parmesan cheese in a small bowl. Spread 1½ tsp. butter mixture on 1 side of 8 Italian bread slices. Place 4 bread slices, buttered sides down, on wax paper. Top each bread slice with 1 (¾-oz.) provolone cheese slice and 1 (¾-oz.) mozzarella cheese slice; top with remaining bread slices, buttered sides up. Cook sandwiches on a hot griddle or in a nonstick skillet over medium heat 4 minutes on each side or until golden brown and cheese is melted.

Fresh Pear-and-Green Bean Salad

MAKES 8 SERVINGS   **HANDS-ON TIME** 15 MIN.   **TOTAL TIME** 20 MIN.

¼ cup sorghum syrup

2 Tbsp. Demerara sugar

½ tsp. kosher salt

¼ tsp. ground red pepper

2 cups pecan halves

Parchment paper

½ cup sorghum syrup

½ cup malt or apple cider vinegar

3 Tbsp. bourbon

2 tsp. grated onion

1 tsp. table salt

1 tsp. freshly ground black pepper

½ tsp. hot sauce

1 cup olive oil

8 oz. haricots verts (tiny green beans), trimmed

1 (5-oz.) package gourmet mixed salad greens

2 red Bartlett pears, cut into thin strips

½ small red onion, sliced

4 oz. Gorgonzola cheese, crumbled

1. Preheat oven to 350°. Stir together first 4 ingredients. Add pecan halves; stir until coated. Place pecans in a single layer on a jelly-roll pan lined with lightly greased parchment paper. Bake for 15 minutes or until glaze bubbles slowly and thickens, stirring once after 8 minutes. Transfer pan to a wire rack. Separate pecans into individual pieces; cool completely in pan. If cooled pecans are not crisp, bake 5 more minutes.

2. Whisk together ½ cup syrup and next 6 ingredients until blended. Add oil in a slow, steady stream, whisking until smooth.

3. Cook beans in boiling salted water to cover 3 to 4 minutes or until crisp-tender; drain. Plunge beans into ice water; drain. Toss together beans, pecans, greens, and next 3 ingredients. Serve with vinaigrette.

QUICK TIP By plunging the green beans in ice water after blanching, you're locking in bright color and flavor.

easy side

Carrot Salad: Combine 2 cups matchstick carrots, ½ cup diced red onion, 4 Tbsp. light red wine vinaigrette, and ½ tsp. freshly ground black pepper in a medium bowl; toss gently.

Roasted Sweet Potato Salad

MAKES 4 TO 6 SERVINGS   **HANDS-ON TIME** 20 MIN.   **TOTAL TIME** 1 HOUR, 5 MIN.

- 1 (24-oz.) package fresh steam-in-bag petite sweet potatoes
- 1 Tbsp. Caribbean jerk seasoning
- 4 Tbsp. olive oil, divided
- 2 Tbsp. fresh lime juice
- ¼ tsp. table salt
- 1 (5-oz.) package baby arugula
- 1 mango, peeled and diced
- 1 avocado, halved and thinly sliced
- ½ red bell pepper, sliced
- ½ small red onion, sliced
- ½ cup torn fresh basil

1. Preheat oven to 425°. Cut potatoes in half lengthwise; toss with jerk seasoning and 1 Tbsp. oil. Arrange, cut sides down, in a single layer on a lightly greased baking sheet. Bake for 15 minutes; turn and bake 8 to 10 more minutes or until tender. Cool on a wire rack 20 minutes.

2. Whisk together lime juice, salt, and remaining 3 Tbsp. oil in a large bowl. Add arugula and next 5 ingredients, and toss to coat. Arrange on a platter; top with potatoes.

QUICK TIP 24 oz. coarsely chopped sweet potatoes can be substituted for petite sweet potatoes.

make ahead

Prepare recipe as directed through Step 1. Cover potatoes and chill up to one day ahead before assembling salad.

BLT Salad

MAKES 4 SERVINGS   **HANDS-ON TIME** 30 MIN.   **TOTAL TIME** 40 MIN.

We reinvented the classic BLT into a salad complete with a tangy garlicky mayo-based dressing.

- 6 **artisan bread slices, halved**
- 2 **Tbsp. extra virgin olive oil**
- 1 **tsp. kosher salt, divided**
- 1 **tsp. freshly ground black pepper, divided**
- 6 **thick applewood-smoked bacon slices, chopped**
- 1 **sweet onion, halved and sliced**
- 1 **garlic clove**
- ½ **cup mayonnaise**
- 2 **Tbsp. fresh lemon juice**
- 1 **lb. assorted heirloom tomatoes, cut into wedges**
- 1 **(5-oz.) package arugula**

1. Preheat oven to 400°. Drizzle bread with oil; sprinkle with ½ tsp. each salt and pepper. Bake in a single layer in a jelly-roll pan 12 minutes or until golden.

2. Cook bacon in a skillet over medium heat, stirring occasionally, 10 minutes or until crisp. Drain on paper towels; reserve 1 Tbsp. drippings in skillet.

3. Sauté onion in hot drippings over medium-low heat 3 to 5 minutes or until tender.

4. Smash garlic to make a paste. Whisk together mayonnaise, lemon juice, garlic paste, and remaining ½ tsp. each salt and pepper.

5. Toss together tomatoes, arugula, bacon, onion, and salt and pepper to taste in a large bowl. Pour mayonnaise mixture over tomato mixture, and toss to coat. Serve immediately.

QUICK TIP Vary the color and type of tomatoes you use. Your salad will be all the more vibrant and flavorful.

easy side

Sweet Potato Fries with Rosemary Ketchup: Prepare frozen sweet potato fries according to package directions. Meanwhile, stir together 1 (14.5-oz.) can fire-roasted diced tomatoes with garlic, drained; ½ cup ketchup; 1 garlic clove, minced; and ½ tsp. dried rosemary. Serve with fries.

Harvest Salad

MAKES 6 TO 8 SERVINGS **HANDS-ON TIME** 20 MIN. **TOTAL TIME** 50 MIN.

- 1 large butternut squash
- 2 Tbsp. olive oil
- 2 Tbsp. honey
- 1 tsp. kosher salt
- ½ tsp. freshly ground black pepper
- 1 (8-oz.) bottle poppy-seed dressing
- ¼ cup fresh or frozen cranberries
- 2 (4-oz.) packages gourmet mixed salad greens
- 4 oz. goat cheese, crumbled
- ¾ cup lightly salted, roasted pecan halves
- 6 bacon slices, cooked and crumbled

1. Preheat oven to 400°. Peel and seed butternut squash; cut into ¾-inch cubes. Toss together squash, olive oil, and next 3 ingredients in a large bowl; place in a single layer in a lightly greased aluminum foil-lined 15- x 10-inch jelly-roll pan.

2. Bake at 400° for 20 to 25 minutes or until squash is tender and begins to brown, stirring once after 10 minutes. Remove from oven, and cool in pan 10 minutes.

3. Meanwhile, pulse poppy-seed dressing and cranberries in a blender 3 to 4 times or until cranberries are coarsely chopped.

4. Toss together squash, gourmet salad greens, and next 3 ingredients on a large serving platter. Serve with dressing.

QUICK TIP Fresh cranberries add sweet-tart fall flavor to bottled dressing.

easy side

Cheesy Garlic Bread:
Preheat broiler with oven rack 5 inches from heat. Cut 2 (6-oz.) French bread baguettes in half lengthwise. Spread 1 garlic clove, pressed, on cut sides of bread; brush with 3 Tbsp. olive oil vinaigrette. Top with 1 tsp. chopped fresh rosemary and ½ cup finely grated Asiago cheese. Broil 4 minutes or until cheese melts and bread is lightly browned. Cut into 16 pieces.

Grilled Shrimp Salad

MAKES 8 SERVINGS   **HANDS-ON TIME** 35 MIN.
TOTAL TIME 1 HOUR, 10 MIN., INCLUDING BASIL VINAIGRETTE

- 8 (12-inch) wooden skewers
- 2 lb. peeled and deveined large raw shrimp
- Basil Vinaigrette, divided
- 2 (6-oz.) packages fresh baby spinach
- 2 mangoes, peeled and sliced
- 1 small red onion, halved and sliced
- 1 (4-oz.) package goat cheese, crumbled
- 1 cup fresh raspberries

1. Soak wooden skewers in water to cover 30 minutes. Meanwhile, preheat grill to 350° to 400° (medium-high) heat. Combine shrimp and ¾ cup Basil Vinaigrette in a large zip-top plastic freezer bag; seal and chill 15 minutes, turning occasionally. Remove shrimp from marinade, discarding marinade. Thread shrimp onto skewers. Grill shrimp, covered with grill lid, 2 minutes on each side or just until shrimp turn pink. Remove shrimp from skewers.

2. Toss spinach, mangoes, and onion with ¼ cup Basil Vinaigrette in a bowl; arrange on a platter. Top with grilled shrimp. Sprinkle with goat cheese and raspberries. Serve with remaining vinaigrette.

Basil Vinaigrette

MAKES 1½ CUPS   **HANDS-ON TIME** 5 MIN.   **TOTAL TIME** 5 MIN.

Whisk together ½ cup chopped fresh basil, ½ cup raspberry vinegar, 2 minced garlic cloves, 1 Tbsp. brown sugar, 2 tsp. Dijon mustard, ½ tsp. table salt, and ½ tsp. dried crushed red pepper until blended. Add 1 cup olive oil in a slow, steady stream, whisking constantly until smooth.

QUICK TIP Raspberries are a surprisingly great combination with fresh basil, mangoes, and shrimp in this summery salad.

make ahead

Prepare recipe as directed through Step 2. Cover and refrigerate shrimp for up to 1 day ahead. Assemble salad with chilled shrimp or warm shrimp before topping salad.

Spring Salmon and Vegetable Salad

MAKES 4 TO 6 SERVINGS   **HANDS-ON TIME** 20 MIN.
TOTAL TIME 30 MIN., INCLUDING CREAMY HERB DRESSING

- ½ lb. fresh asparagus, cut into 1-inch pieces
- 1 cup sugar snap peas
- 1¼ lb. skinless salmon fillets, cut into 2-inch chunks
- ½ tsp. table salt
- ¼ tsp. freshly ground black pepper
- 6 cups chopped romaine lettuce hearts
- ½ cup uncooked shelled fresh or frozen edamame, thawed
- ¼ cup sliced radishes
- **Creamy Herb Dressing**

1. Preheat broiler with oven rack 6 inches from heat. Cook asparagus with sugar snap peas in boiling salted water 2 to 3 minutes or until crisp-tender; drain. Plunge into ice water to stop the cooking process; drain.

2. Sprinkle salmon with salt and pepper; broil on a lightly greased rack in a broiler pan 3 to 4 minutes or to desired degree of doneness.

3. Arrange lettuce, edamame, radishes, asparagus mixture, and salmon on a serving plate. Drizzle with dressing.

Creamy Herb Dressing

MAKES 1 CUP   **HANDS-ON TIME** 5 MIN.   **TOTAL TIME** 5 MIN.

- ½ cup buttermilk
- ¼ cup mayonnaise
- 3 Tbsp. chopped fresh herbs (such as mint, dill, and chives)
- 1 Tbsp. fresh lemon juice

Whisk together all ingredients, and salt and pepper to taste. Chill 30 minutes.

> **QUICK TIP** For easy cleanup, line your broiler pan with foil before broiling salmon.

make ahead

Creamy Herb Dressing will keep for up to one week in the refrigerator.

Warm Barbecue Salad

MAKES 6 SERVINGS   **HANDS-ON TIME** 10 MIN.
TOTAL TIME 1 HOUR, 5 MIN., INCLUDING BARBECUE DRESSING

  3 cups shredded smoked pork
Barbecue Dressing, divided
  1 cup frozen whole kernel corn, thawed
  2 bacon slices, cooked and crumbled
  1 (8-oz.) bag mixed salad greens
  4 plum tomatoes, chopped
  ⅓ large red onion, sliced
  ⅔ cup shredded mozzarella cheese

1. Preheat oven to 350°. Stir together pork and 1 cup Barbecue Dressing in a lightly greased 9-inch square pan.

2. Bake, covered, at 350° for 35 minutes or until warm.

3. Toss together corn and next 4 ingredients. Top with warm barbecue mixture, and sprinkle with cheese. Serve immediately with remaining dressing.

Barbecue Dressing

MAKES 3 CUPS   **HANDS-ON TIME** 10 MIN.   **TOTAL TIME** 20 MIN.

  1 (18-oz.) bottle barbecue sauce
  ⅓ cup firmly packed light brown sugar
  ½ cup honey
  ⅓ cup ketchup
  1 Tbsp. butter
  1 Tbsp. Worcestershire sauce
  ½ tsp. seasoned salt
  1 tsp. lemon pepper

Stir together all ingredients in a saucepan; bring to a boil. Reduce heat; simmer, stirring occasionally, 10 minutes.

QUICK TIP If you can't find smoked pork at your grocery, you can buy it by the pound at a BBQ restaurant.

easy side

Jerk-Spiced Sweet Potato Fries: Coat frozen sweet potato fries with olive oil and Jamaican jerk seasoning; bake according to package directions.

QUICK TIP **Cooking the ham hocks the day before and chilling the soup overnight will allow you to skim the fat easily.**

easy side

Cornbread Croutons:

Preheat oven to 450°. Coat bottom and sides of an 8-inch square pan with 2 Tbsp. bacon drippings; heat in oven 5 minutes. Whisk together 1 cup cornmeal mix, 1 cup buttermilk, 1 large egg, ¼ tsp. table salt, and ¼ tsp. black pepper; pour batter into hot pan. Bake 15 to 17 minutes or until lightly browned. Turn out onto a wire rack; cool completely. Reduce oven temperature to 325°. Cut cornbread into 1 ½-inch squares. Place on a baking sheet; sprinkle with ¼ tsp. table salt and ¼ tsp. pepper. Bake at 325° for 30 to 35 minutes or until crisp and lightly browned. Remove to a wire rack; cool completely.

Pot Likker Soup

MAKES 6 TO 8 SERVINGS   **HANDS-ON TIME** 20 MIN.
TOTAL TIME 12 HOURS, 53 MIN.

2 (1-lb.) smoked ham hocks
1 medium onion, chopped
1 medium carrot, diced
1 Tbsp. vegetable oil
1 garlic clove, chopped
½ cup dry white wine
½ tsp. table salt
¼ tsp. dried crushed red pepper
1 (14.5-oz.) can vegetable broth
½ (16-oz.) package fresh collard greens, washed and trimmed

1. Bring ham hocks and 8 cups water to a boil in a Dutch oven over medium-high heat. Boil 5 minutes; drain. Reserve hocks; wipe Dutch oven clean.

2. Sauté onion and carrot in hot oil in Dutch oven over medium heat 4 to 5 minutes or until tender; add garlic, and cook 1 minute. Add wine; cook, stirring occasionally, 2 minutes or until wine is reduced by half.

3. Add hocks, 8 cups water, salt, and red pepper to onion mixture, and bring to a boil. Cover, reduce heat to low, and simmer 3 hours or until ham hocks are tender.

4. Remove hocks, and cool 30 minutes. Remove meat from bones; discard bones. Transfer meat to an airtight container; cover and chill. Cover Dutch oven with lid, and chill soup 8 hours.

5. Skim and discard fat from soup in Dutch oven. Stir in meat and vegetable broth.

6. Bring mixture to a boil. Gradually stir in collards. Reduce heat, and simmer, stirring occasionally, 45 to 50 minutes or until collards are tender.

Spinach-Bacon Mac and Cheese

MAKES 4 SERVINGS   **HANDS-ON TIME** 20 MIN.   **TOTAL TIME** 20 MIN.

Take rotini and a homemade cheese sauce, add some bacon, and your little ones won't even notice they're eating spinach when they dig into this delicious meal.

- ½ (16-oz.) package rotini pasta
- ¼ cup butter
- ¼ cup all-purpose flour
- 2½ cups 2% reduced-fat milk
- ½ tsp. table salt
- ¼ tsp. ground red pepper
- ⅛ tsp. garlic powder
- 1 (10-oz.) block 2% sharp Cheddar cheese, shredded
- ½ cup chopped cooked bacon (about 6 slices)
- 1 (6-oz.) package fresh baby spinach

1. Prepare pasta according to package directions.

2. Meanwhile, melt butter in a large saucepan over medium heat. Gradually whisk in flour until smooth; cook, whisking constantly, 1 minute. Gradually whisk in milk and next 3 ingredients; cook, whisking constantly, 8 to 10 minutes or until thickened. Remove from heat.

3. Gradually stir in Cheddar cheese, stirring until cheese is melted and sauce is smooth. Stir in bacon, spinach, and hot cooked pasta. Serve immediately.

QUICK TIP It may look like too much spinach, but it will wilt down with the hot pasta.

easy side

Italian-Seasoned Bread: Preheat oven to 350°. Split 1 (12-oz.) French bread loaf lengthwise, and brush cut sides with ½ cup melted butter. Top with 6 garlic cloves, pressed; 1 tsp. dried oregano; and ½ tsp. dried parsley flakes. Bake for 8 to 10 minutes until lightly browned and crisp.

From salads to casseroles, rotisserie chicken makes dinner a cinch and gives any dish from-scratch flavor.

CHICKEN-AND-TORTELLINI SALAD, PAGE 126 ▶

Strawberry Chicken Salad

MAKES ABOUT 7 CUPS   **HANDS-ON TIME** 20 MIN.   **TOTAL TIME** 2 HOURS, 20 MIN.

This is the quintessential spring salad, celebrating the sweet taste of the season with fresh strawberries and fresh-from-the-garden basil.

- ½ cup bottled poppy-seed dressing
- ¼ cup minced green onions
- 3 Tbsp. chopped fresh basil
- ½ tsp. freshly ground pepper
- 4 cups chopped rotisserie chicken
- 2 cups diced fresh strawberries
- 1 cup chopped toasted pecans
- **Romaine lettuce leaves**

Stir together poppy-seed dressing and next 3 ingredients in a large bowl. Fold in chicken and strawberries; add salt to taste. Cover and chill 2 hours. Stir in pecans just before serving. Serve over romaine lettuce leaves.

QUICK TIP Fresh strawberries are available year-round, but they're best from April to June.

easy side

▶ **Grilled Pimiento Cheese:** Spread deli pimiento cheese on 1 side of a white bread slice; top with another bread slice. Lightly spread both sides of sandwich with mayonnaise. Repeat with remaining pimiento cheese and bread for desired number of sandwiches. Cook, in batches, on a hot griddle or a large nonstick skillet over medium heat 4 to 5 minutes on each side or until golden brown and cheese melts.

Mixed Fruit Chicken Salad

MAKES 7 SERVINGS   HANDS-ON TIME 30 MIN.
TOTAL TIME 45 MIN., INCLUDING ORANGE-RASPBERRY VINAIGRETTE

- 4 cups chopped rotisserie chicken breasts
- 2 cups seedless red and green grapes, halved
- 2 celery ribs, chopped
- 1 (11-oz.) can mandarin oranges, drained
- 1 cup chopped fresh pineapple*
- ¼ tsp. table salt
  Orange-Raspberry Vinaigrette
- ¼ cup chopped toasted pecans

Toss together chicken and next 5 ingredients in a large bowl. Add vinaigrette; toss to coat. Sprinkle with pecans, and serve immediately.

*1 (8-oz.) can pineapple tidbits, drained, may be substituted.

Orange-Raspberry Vinaigrette

MAKES 1 CUP   HANDS-ON TIME 10 MIN.   TOTAL TIME 10 MIN.

- ½ cup orange marmalade
- ¼ cup white balsamic-raspberry blush vinegar
- 1 medium-size jalapeño pepper, seeded and minced
- 2 Tbsp. chopped fresh cilantro
- 2 Tbsp. olive oil

Whisk together all ingredients.

QUICK TIP For extra fiber and a boost of antioxidants, serve chicken salad over dark greens.

make ahead

The vinaigrette can be made up to a week ahead and chilled until ready to use.

Chicken-and-Wild Rice Salad

MAKES 6 SERVINGS   **HANDS-ON TIME** 15 MIN.   **TOTAL TIME** 15 MIN.

- 3 Tbsp. soy sauce
- 3 Tbsp. rice wine vinegar
- 2 Tbsp. sesame oil
- 1 (8.5-oz.) pouch ready-to-serve whole grain brown and wild rice mix
- 3 cups shredded rotisserie chicken
- 1 cup diced red bell pepper
- 1 cup chopped toasted pecans
- 1 cup baby spinach
- ¼ cup minced green onions

1. Whisk together first 3 ingredients in a large bowl.

2. Prepare brown and wild rice mix according to package directions. Stir chicken, next 4 ingredients, and rice into soy sauce mixture. Add freshly ground pepper to taste.

QUICK TIP Sold washed and bagged, baby spinach is a bright and flavorful addition to chicken salad.

make ahead

Prepare recipe as directed without adding spinach and pecans up to 1 day ahead. Stir in watercress and pecans just before serving.

Chutney Chicken Salad

MAKES 8 SERVINGS   **HANDS-ON TIME** 30 MIN.   **TOTAL TIME** 2 HOURS, 50 MIN.

If you love curry powder, feel free to add more. The mango chutney, curry, and almonds are a bold twist on the traditional chicken salad.

- 1 **cup mayonnaise**
- ½ **cup Greek yogurt**
- ⅓ **cup mango chutney**
- 1 **Tbsp. curry powder**
- 1 **tsp. table salt**
- ¼ **tsp. freshly ground black pepper**
- 5 **cups diced rotisserie chicken**
- ⅓ **cup slivered toasted almonds**
- 1 **(8-oz.) can sliced water chestnuts, drained**
- 4 **green onions, chopped (about 1 cup)**
- ½ **(14.1-oz.) package refrigerated piecrusts**
- **Garnish: thinly sliced green onions**

1. Whisk together mayonnaise and next 5 ingredients in a large bowl. Add chicken and next 3 ingredients, and toss until well blended. Cover and chill 2 to 24 hours.

2. Preheat oven to 450°. Cut piecrust into 8 (4½-inch) rounds. Press each dough round into a lightly greased 3½-inch brioche mold, pressing dough up sides. Fold dough over edge of molds, and pinch to secure. Arrange molds on a baking sheet.

3. Bake at 450° for 8 minutes or until lightly browned. Cool pastry shells in molds on a wire rack 1 minute. Loosen shells from molds using a small knife; remove shells from molds to wire racks, and cool completely (about 20 minutes).

4. Fill cooled pastry shells with chicken salad just before serving.

QUICK TIP Try using tart pans and brioche molds in different shapes and sizes for an array of pretty tartlets.

make ahead

Prepare chicken salad as directed up to 1 day in advance. Fill shells just before serving.

Chicken Salad Pitas

MAKES 4 DOZEN **HANDS-ON TIME** 30 MIN. **TOTAL TIME** 4 HOURS, 30 MIN.

*Great for a luncheon or as heavy hors d'oeuvres,
these little pita pockets pack a punch of flavor with
red pepper jelly, cilantro, and fresh lime.*

- ½ cup mayonnaise
- ⅓ cup red pepper jelly
- ¼ cup minced green onions
- 2 Tbsp. chopped fresh cilantro
- 1 tsp. lime zest
- ¼ tsp. ground red pepper
- 2 cups finely chopped rotisserie chicken
- ½ cup finely chopped celery
- ½ cup finely chopped toasted pecans
- 24 mini pita pockets, halved
- 1 bunch fresh watercress

1. Whisk together first 6 ingredients in a large bowl; stir in chicken and next 2 ingredients until blended. Season with salt and black pepper to taste.

2. Cover and chill 4 hours. Fill pitas with watercress and chicken salad. Serve immediately.

QUICK TIP This chicken salad is a little spicy. If you want to dial down the heat, omit ground red pepper.

make ahead

You can make the chicken salad a day ahead of time. Just keep refrigerated until ready to serve. Fill the pitas just before serving.

Chicken-and-Tortellini Salad

MAKES 6 SERVINGS   **HANDS-ON TIME** 20 MIN.   **TOTAL TIME** 30 MIN.

2 (9-oz.) packages refrigerated cheese-filled tortellini

½ cup olive oil

½ cup grated Parmesan cheese

¼ cup fresh lemon juice

2 garlic cloves

1 tsp. Worcestershire sauce

2 cups chopped rotisserie chicken

1 cup frozen sweet peas, thawed

½ cup thinly sliced green onions

½ cup chopped fresh flat-leaf parsley

1. Prepare pasta according to package directions.

2. Process olive oil and next 4 ingredients in a blender until smooth. Toss olive oil mixture with pasta, chicken, and next 3 ingredients. Add salt and pepper to taste.

QUICK TIP The hot tortellini will warm the chicken and peas when tossed together.

easy side

Spinach-and-Red Pepper Sauté: Sauté ¼ cup pine nuts in 1 Tbsp. hot olive oil in a nonstick skillet over medium-high heat 4 minutes or until golden. Remove from skillet. Sauté 3 (10-oz.) packages fresh spinach and 2 garlic cloves, pressed, over medium-high heat 4 to 5 minutes or until spinach wilts. Drain well. Stir in pine nuts; ½ (12-oz.) jar roasted red bell peppers, drained and chopped; ½ tsp. table salt; and ¼ tsp. pepper.

Baked Chicken Risotto

MAKES 4 SERVINGS   **HANDS-ON TIME** 20 MIN.   **TOTAL TIME** 1 HOUR

- 3 Tbsp. butter
- 1 cup minced sweet onion
- 2 garlic cloves, pressed
- 1 cup Arborio rice (short-grain)
- ¼ cup dry white wine
- 4 cups chicken broth
- 1 (14-oz.) can quartered artichoke hearts, drained
- 3 cups chopped rotisserie chicken
- 2 medium zucchini, coarsely chopped (about 2 cups)
- ½ tsp. freshly ground black pepper
- ½ cup grated Parmesan cheese
- ¼ cup chopped fresh parsley
- 1 tsp. lemon zest

1. Preheat oven to 425°. Melt butter in a Dutch oven over medium-high heat; add onion and garlic, and sauté 5 minutes. Add rice, and cook 2 minutes or until golden brown. Add wine, and cook 2 to 3 minutes or until wine is absorbed. Add chicken broth. Bring to a boil, cover, and transfer to oven. Bake for 20 minutes.

2. Remove rice from oven, and stir in artichokes and next 3 ingredients. Cover and bake 10 more minutes. Remove from oven, and let stand 5 minutes. Stir in cheese and remaining ingredients. Serve immediately.

QUICK TIP For creamy texture, never rinse rice before cooking risotto, and be sure to use a short-grain rice such as Arborio.

easy side

Nutty Green Beans:
Cook 1 (12-oz.) package frozen steam-in-bag whole green beans according to package directions. Toss with 1 Tbsp. each butter, lemon zest, and lemon juice. Sprinkle with 3 Tbsp. roasted pecan-and-almond pieces; add salt and pepper to taste.

Chicken Enchiladas

MAKES 6 TO 8 SERVINGS **HANDS-ON TIME** 25 MIN.
TOTAL TIME 2 HOURS, 45 MIN.

- 1 cup diced sweet onion
- 3 garlic cloves, minced
- 1 Tbsp. canola oil
- 2 cups chopped fresh baby spinach
- 2 (4.5-oz.) cans chopped green chiles, drained
- 3 cups shredded rotisserie chicken
- 1 (8-oz.) package ⅓-less-fat cream cheese, cubed and softened
- 2 cups (8 oz.) shredded pepper Jack cheese
- ⅓ cup chopped fresh cilantro
- 8 (8-inch) soft taco-size flour tortillas

Vegetable cooking spray

1. Preheat oven to 350°. Sauté onion and garlic in hot oil in a large skillet over medium heat 5 minutes or until tender. Add spinach and green chiles; sauté 1 to 2 minutes or until spinach is wilted. Stir in chicken and next 3 ingredients, and cook, stirring constantly, 5 minutes or until cheeses melt. Add salt and pepper to taste. Spoon about ¾ cup chicken mixture down center of each tortilla; roll up tortillas.

2. Place rolled tortillas, seam sides down, in a lightly greased 13- x 9-inch baking dish. Lightly coat tortillas with cooking spray.

3. Bake at 350° for 30 to 35 minutes or until golden brown.

QUICK TIP Purchase tomatillos with dry, tight-fitting husks for the longest shelf life.

easy side

▶ **Tomatillo Salsa:**
Stir together 2 cups diced tomatillo, ⅓ cup sliced green onions, ⅓ cup lightly packed fresh cilantro leaves, 1 seeded and minced jalapeño pepper, 1 Tbsp. fresh lime juice, and ½ tsp. table salt. Cover and chill 1 to 4 hours. Let stand at room temperature 30 minutes. Stir in 1 cup diced avocado just before serving. Spoon on top of Chicken Enchiladas.

Chicken-and-Wild Rice Casserole

MAKES 10 TO 12 SERVINGS **HANDS-ON TIME** 30 MIN.
TOTAL TIME 1 HOUR, 15 MIN.

Using a long-grain and wild rice mix and toasted almonds in chicken casserole makes it a little bit dressier and fit for company during the holidays.

- 2 (6.2-oz.) boxes fast-cooking long-grain and wild rice mix
- ¼ cup butter
- 4 celery ribs, chopped
- 2 medium onions, chopped
- 5 cups chopped rotisserie chicken
- 2 (10¾-oz.) cans cream of mushroom soup
- 2 (8-oz.) cans chopped water chestnuts, drained
- 1 (8-oz.) container sour cream
- 1 cup milk
- ½ tsp. table salt
- ½ tsp. black pepper
- 4 cups (16 oz.) shredded Cheddar cheese, divided
- 2 cups soft, fresh breadcrumbs
- 1 (2.25-oz.) package sliced toasted almonds

1. Preheat oven to 350°. Prepare rice mixes according to package directions.

2. Meanwhile, melt butter in a large skillet over medium heat; add celery and onions. Sauté 10 minutes or until tender. Stir in chicken, next 6 ingredients, rice, and 3 cups cheese. Spoon mixture into a lightly greased 15- x 10-inch baking dish or 2 (11- x 7-inch) baking dishes. Top with breadcrumbs.

3. Bake at 350° for 35 minutes. Sprinkle with remaining 1 cup cheese, and top with toasted almonds. Bake 5 more minutes.

QUICK TIP Store fresh breadcrumbs in the refrigerator in a tightly sealed container for 1 week, or freeze up to 6 months.

make ahead

Prepare as directed through Step 2. Cover with aluminum foil, and freeze up to 1 month. Remove from freezer, and let stand at room temperature 1 hour. Bake casserole, covered, at 350° for 30 minutes. Uncover and bake 55 more minutes to 1 hour and 15 minutes or until thoroughly heated. Sprinkle with 1 cup (4 oz.) shredded Cheddar cheese and toasted almonds. Bake 5 more minutes.

Mexican Chicken Casserole

MAKES 8 SERVINGS　**HANDS-ON TIME** 10 MIN.　**TOTAL TIME** 4 HOURS, 10 MIN.

The corn tortillas cook into this dish and thicken it—you won't see them after they're cooked, but you will still taste their authentic Mexican flavor.

- 2　(10-oz.) cans mild green chile enchilada sauce
- 10　(6-inch) corn tortillas, torn into 3-inch pieces
- 4　cups shredded rotisserie chicken
- 1½　cups sour cream
- 1　(12-oz.) package shredded colby-Jack cheese blend, divided
- 1　(10¾-oz.) can cream of mushroom soup
- 8　cups shredded iceberg lettuce
- 1　(15-oz.) can black beans
- 3　tomatoes, diced

1. Spoon ½ cup enchilada sauce over bottom of a greased 4-qt. slow cooker. Add enough tortilla pieces to cover sauce.

2. Stir together chicken, sour cream, 2 cups cheese, and soup. Spread 2 cups chicken mixture over tortilla pieces. Top with tortilla pieces to cover. Drizzle with ½ cup enchilada sauce. Repeat layers twice, ending with tortilla pieces and remaining enchilada sauce. Sprinkle with remaining 1 cup cheese.

3. Cover and cook on LOW 4 hours. Place lettuce on 8 individual plates; top each evenly with chicken enchilada mixture, beans, and tomatoes. Serve immediately.

QUICK TIP Don't throw away leftover tortillas; cut them into triangles or strips, and fry or bake them to top a salad or soup.

easy side

Dressed-up Refried Beans: Preheat oven to 450°. Combine 2 (20.5-oz.) cans refried black beans, ½ (8-oz.) package whipped chive-flavored cream cheese, and ½ tsp. ground cumin in a 2-qt. baking dish. Top with 2 Tbsp. finely chopped red onion and 1 cup crumbled queso fresco (fresh Mexican cheese). Bake for 20 to 30 minutes or until cheese melts.

Chicken and Cranberry Dressing

MAKES 8 TO 10 SERVINGS   **HANDS-ON TIME** 15 MIN.
TOTAL TIME 7 HOURS, 15 MIN.

- 1 slow-cooker liner
- Vegetable cooking spray
- 6 cups crumbled cornbread
- 4 cups chopped or shredded rotisserie chicken
- 2 cups frozen chopped celery, onion, and bell pepper mix
- 1½ cups dried cranberries or cherries
- 8 slices firm white bread, torn into bite-size pieces
- 3 large eggs, lightly beaten
- 2 (14-oz.) cans chicken broth
- 2 (10¾-oz.) cans cream of chicken soup
- ½ tsp. freshly ground black pepper
- ⅓ cup butter, cut into pieces
- Garnish: whole-berry cranberry sauce

1. Place a slow-cooker liner in a 5- or 6-qt. slow cooker. Coat liner with cooking spray. Place cornbread in liner. Add chicken and next 7 ingredients; toss gently. Dot with butter.

2. Cover and cook on HIGH 4 hours or on LOW 7 hours or until dressing is puffed and set in center. Rotate slow cooker insert halfway after 2 hours. Stir before serving.

QUICK TIP Chopped cooked turkey is a great substitute for rotisserie chicken in this recipe.

make ahead

Prepare recipe as directed through Step 1. Cover and refrigerate slow cooker insert up to 8 hours. Continue with recipe as directed, cooking an additional 1 hour, if necessary.

Swiss Chicken Crêpes

MAKES 4 TO 6 SERVINGS   **HANDS-ON TIME** 20 MIN.
TOTAL TIME 1 HOUR, 5 MIN.

- ⅓ cup dry vermouth
- 1 garlic clove, pressed
- 3 cups half-and-half
- 3 Tbsp. cornstarch
- 1 tsp. table salt
- ½ tsp. black pepper
- 3 cups (12 oz.) shredded Swiss cheese, divided
- 1 (12-oz.) jar roasted red bell peppers, drained
- 3 cups finely chopped rotisserie chicken
- 1 (5-oz.) package fresh baby spinach, chopped
- ¼ cup chopped fresh basil
- 1 garlic clove, pressed
- 1 tsp. seasoned pepper
- 8 egg roll wrappers

Garnish: fresh basil leaves

1. Preheat oven to 350°. Bring vermouth and garlic to a boil in a large skillet over medium-high heat; reduce heat to medium-low, and simmer 7 to 10 minutes or until vermouth is reduced to 1 Tbsp. Whisk together half-and-half and cornstarch. Whisk salt, black pepper, and half-and-half mixture into vermouth mixture; bring to a boil over medium-high heat, whisking constantly. Boil, whisking constantly, 1 minute or until mixture is thickened. Add 2 cups cheese; reduce heat to low, and simmer, whisking constantly, 1 minute or until cheese is melted and sauce is smooth. Remove from heat.

2. Process peppers in a blender until smooth. Pour into 4 lightly greased 7- x 4½-inch baking dishes.

3. Stir together remaining 1 cup cheese, chicken, next 4 ingredients, and 1 cup cheese sauce. Divide chicken mixture among wrappers, spooning down centers; gently roll up. Place, seam sides down, over red pepper puree in baking dishes. Top with remaining cheese sauce. Cover with aluminum foil. Bake, covered, at 350° for 15 minutes or until thoroughly heated and bubbly.

QUICK TIP This recipe uses egg roll wrappers instead of crêpes, making for a quick weeknight dinner.

make ahead

Prepare recipe as directed through Step 2. Cover and refrigerate up to 8 hours. Continue with recipe as directed, baking an additional 10 minutes, or until heated through and bubbly.

Chicken Pot Pie with Cheddar Biscuits

MAKES 6 TO 8 SERVINGS   **HANDS-ON TIME** 50 MIN.
TOTAL TIME 1 HOUR, 30 MIN.

Cheesy biscuits replace the traditional pastry crust in this pot pie.

- ⅓ cup butter
- ⅓ cup all-purpose flour
- 1½ cups chicken broth
- 1½ cups milk
- 1½ tsp. Creole seasoning
- 2 Tbsp. butter
- 1 large sweet onion, diced
- 1 (8-oz.) package sliced fresh mushrooms
- 4 cups shredded rotisserie chicken
- 2 cups frozen cubed hash browns, thawed
- 2 carrots, sliced diagonally
- 1 cup frozen small sweet peas
- 1 (16.3-oz.) can butter-flavored biscuits
- ½ cup (2 oz.) shredded sharp Cheddar cheese
- ¼ cup finely chopped cooked bacon

1. Preheat oven to 425°. Melt ⅓ cup butter in a large saucepan over medium heat; add flour, and cook, whisking constantly, 1 minute. Gradually add chicken broth and milk, and cook, whisking constantly, 6 to 7 minutes or until thickened and bubbly. Remove from heat, and stir in Creole seasoning.

2. Melt 2 Tbsp. butter in a large Dutch oven over medium-high heat; add onion and mushrooms, and sauté 10 minutes or until tender. Stir in chicken, next 3 ingredients, and sauce. Spoon filling into a lightly greased 13- x 9-inch baking dish.

3. Bake at 425° for 15 minutes. Remove from oven, and arrange biscuits over hot chicken mixture. Bake for 20 to 25 more minutes or until biscuits are golden brown and chicken mixture is bubbly. Remove from oven and top with Cheddar cheese and bacon.

QUICK TIP Feel free to use your favorite refrigerated biscuit for this recipe. Just be sure to buy enough to cover the top of the dish.

make ahead

Prepare recipe as directed through Step 2. Cover and refrigerate up to 1 day ahead. Uncover and continue with recipe as directed.

Buy chicken breasts in bulk when they're on sale, and use them up with this great mix of recipes from soups and kabobs to stir-fry and sandwiches.

BAKED CHICKEN ROULADE, PAGE 166 ▶

Smoky Chicken Panini with Basil Mayo

MAKES 4 SERVINGS   **HANDS-ON TIME** 35 MIN.   **TOTAL TIME** 45 MIN.

Smoky Gouda cheese, sun-dried tomatoes, and baby spinach join grilled chicken breasts in this panini that's slathered with fresh Basil Mayo.

- 4 skinned and boned chicken breasts (about 1 lb.)
- ½ tsp. table salt
- ⅛ tsp. freshly ground pepper
- ½ cup mayonnaise
- 2 Tbsp. chopped fresh basil
- ½ tsp. lemon zest
- 8 sourdough bread slices
- ½ lb. smoked Gouda cheese, sliced
- 1 cup loosely packed baby spinach
- ¼ cup thinly sliced sun-dried tomatoes
- 3 Tbsp. butter, melted

1. Preheat grill to 350° to 400° (medium-high) heat. Sprinkle chicken with salt and pepper. Grill chicken, covered with grill lid, 7 to 10 minutes on each side or until done. Let stand 10 minutes, and cut into slices.

2. Stir together mayonnaise and next 2 ingredients. Spread mixture on 1 side of each bread slice. Top 4 bread slices with chicken, Gouda, and next 2 ingredients. Top with remaining bread slices, mayonnaise mixture sides down. Brush sandwiches with melted butter.

3. Cook sandwiches, in batches, in a preheated panini press 2 to 3 minutes or until golden brown.

QUICK TIP Store leftover Basil Mayo in the fridge to spice up any sandwich, from turkey to grilled cheese.

easy side

▶ **Apple Salad:**
Combine 4 large Granny Smith apples, chopped; ½ cup sweetened dried cranberries; ⅓ cup light mayonnaise; 2 Tbsp. fresh lemon juice; and ⅛ tsp. salt in a medium bowl; sprinkle with 5 Tbsp. toasted chopped walnuts. Cover and chill until ready to serve.

Pan-Grilled Chicken with Fresh Plum Salsa

MAKES 4 SERVINGS   **HANDS-ON TIME** 26 MIN.   **TOTAL TIME** 26 MIN.

This sweet and spicy chicken dish starts with fast-cooking chicken cutlets, giving you a leg up on dinner—it's ready in 26 minutes.

- 1 cup chopped ripe plums (about 2 plums)
- 1 small jalapeño pepper, seeded and diced
- 2 Tbsp. chopped fresh basil
- 2 Tbsp. chopped red onion
- 2 tsp. fresh lime juice
- ¾ tsp. table salt, divided
- 2 Tbsp. brown sugar
- ½ tsp. ground cumin
- 4 (4-oz.) chicken breast cutlets
- 2 tsp. olive oil

1. Stir together plums, next 4 ingredients, and ¼ tsp. salt in a medium bowl. Set aside.

2. Stir together brown sugar, cumin, and remaining ½ tsp. salt in a small bowl. Rub chicken with brown sugar mixture.

3. Cook chicken in hot oil in a grill pan or nonstick skillet over medium heat 3 minutes on each side or until done. Serve with plum mixture.

QUICK TIP Make chicken breast cutlets by slicing 2 boneless, skinless chicken breasts in half horizontally, making 4 thin pieces.

easy side

Sautéed Sugar Snap Peas: Cook 1 lb. fresh sugar snap peas in boiling salted water to cover 5 minutes or until crisp-tender. Drain and plunge into ice water to stop the cooking process; drain. Melt 2 Tbsp. butter in a medium skillet over medium-high heat; add peas, and sauté 3 minutes. Season to taste with salt and pepper.

Southern Italian Chicken Soup

MAKES 8 SERVINGS   **HANDS-ON TIME** 45 MIN.   **TOTAL TIME** 50 MIN.

- 1   large onion, diced
- 1   celery rib, thinly sliced
- 2   carrots, chopped
- 1   garlic clove, minced
- 3   Tbsp. olive oil, divided
- 6   cups chicken broth
- 1   (15.5-oz.) can diced tomatoes
- 1   tsp. dried Italian seasoning
- ¼   tsp. dried crushed red pepper
- 4   (6- to 8-oz.) skinned and boned chicken breasts
- ½   tsp. table salt
- ½   tsp. black pepper
- 2   cups sliced fresh okra
- 1   (15.5-oz.) can black-eyed peas, drained and rinsed
- 1   (9-oz.) package refrigerated cheese-filled tortellini

Freshly grated Parmesan cheese

1. Sauté first 4 ingredients in 2 Tbsp. hot oil in a large Dutch oven over medium-high heat 3 to 5 minutes or until tender. Stir in broth and next 3 ingredients; bring to a boil, stirring occasionally. Reduce heat to medium, and simmer, stirring occasionally, 10 minutes.

2. Meanwhile, sprinkle chicken with salt and black pepper. Cook in remaining 1 Tbsp. hot oil in a large nonstick skillet over medium-high heat 5 minutes on each side or until lightly browned. Cool slightly (about 5 minutes); cut into 1-inch pieces.

3. Add okra, black-eyed peas, and chicken to Dutch oven. Simmer, stirring occasionally, 10 minutes or until okra is tender. Add tortellini, and cook, stirring occasionally, 3 minutes or until tortellini is done. Serve with Parmesan cheese.

QUICK TIP To make this even quicker, substitute 1 cup prechopped onion and 2 cups frozen sliced okra.

make ahead

This soup can be made up to one day ahead omitting the pasta. Just reheat to boiling, add tortellini, and cook until done.

Mexican Tomato Soup

MAKES 4 TO 6 SERVINGS   **HANDS-ON TIME** 1 HOUR, 5 MIN.
TOTAL TIME 1 HOUR, 40 MIN.

QUICK TIP Charring the tomatoes adds a smoky, deep flavor to this fresh and spicy soup.

easy side

Southwestern Cornbread:
Prepare 1 (19-oz.) package white cornbread mix according to package directions, stirring 1 cup (4 oz.) freshly shredded Monterey Jack cheese and 1 jalapeño pepper, seeded and finely chopped, into batter.

- 2   medium tomatoes, cored and halved
- 1   onion, chopped
- 1   Tbsp. canola oil
- 2   garlic cloves
- 1   (32-oz.) container chicken broth
- 2   cups low-sodium tomato juice
- 1   bay leaf
- ¼   tsp. ground cumin
- ¼   tsp. ground coriander
- ¼   tsp. ground red pepper
- 1½   lb. skinned and boned chicken breasts, cut into ½-inch-wide strips
- 4   green onions (white part only), thinly sliced
- ½   cup fresh lime juice
- ¼   cup chopped fresh cilantro
- ½   cup (2 oz.) crumbled queso fresco (fresh Mexican cheese)
- 1   medium avocado, chopped
- 1   cup tortilla strips

1. Heat a nonstick skillet over high heat 2 minutes. Add tomato halves, and cook, turning occasionally, 10 minutes or until charred on all sides. (Tomatoes may stick.) Transfer to a food processor.

2. Sauté onion in hot oil over medium heat 3 to 5 minutes or until tender. Add garlic; sauté 2 minutes or until fragrant. Transfer onion mixture to food processor with tomatoes; process until smooth.

3. Cook tomato mixture in a Dutch oven over medium-high heat, stirring occasionally, 5 minutes or until thickened. Stir in broth and next 5 ingredients; bring to a boil. Reduce heat to medium-low, and simmer, partially covered and stirring occasionally, 20 minutes. Add chicken; simmer, stirring occasionally, 5 to 7 minutes or until chicken is done.

4. Discard bay leaf. Stir in green onions and next 2 ingredients. Add salt and pepper to taste. Serve topped with queso fresco, avocado, and tortilla strips.

Pecan-Crusted Chicken and Tortellini with Herbed Butter Sauce

MAKES 4 SERVINGS   **HANDS-ON TIME** 20 MIN.   **TOTAL TIME** 30 MIN.

2 (9-oz.) packages refrigerated cheese-filled tortellini

4 (4-oz.) chicken breast cutlets

½ tsp. table salt

¼ tsp. freshly ground pepper

¾ cup finely chopped pecans

1 large egg, lightly beaten

3 Tbsp. olive oil

½ cup butter

3 garlic cloves, thinly sliced

3 Tbsp. chopped fresh basil

3 Tbsp. chopped fresh parsley

¼ cup (1 oz.) shredded Parmesan cheese

1. Prepare pasta according to package directions.

2. Meanwhile, sprinkle chicken with salt and pepper. Place pecans in a shallow bowl. Place egg in a second bowl. Dip chicken in egg, allowing excess to drip off. Dredge chicken in pecans, pressing firmly to adhere.

3. Cook chicken in hot oil in a large nonstick skillet over medium-high heat 2 minutes on each side or until done. Remove from skillet; wipe skillet clean.

4. Melt butter in skillet over medium heat. Add garlic, and sauté 5 to 7 minutes or until garlic is caramel-colored and butter begins to turn golden brown. Immediately remove from heat, and stir in basil, parsley, and hot cooked pasta. Sprinkle with cheese. Serve immediately with chicken.

QUICK TIP Use a food processor to finely chop pecans. The finer they are, the better they will stick to the chicken.

easy side

Balsamic-Glazed Broccoli: Cook 1 (12-oz.) package fresh broccoli florets according to package directions; keep warm. Combine 1 Tbsp. butter, 1 tsp. lemon zest, 1 tsp. fresh lemon juice, 1 tsp. balsamic vinegar, and ¼ tsp. table salt in a small microwavable bowl. Microwave at HIGH 30 seconds or until butter melts; pour butter mixture over broccoli and toss gently.

Chicken-and-Veggie Stir-fry

MAKES 4 SERVINGS.   **HANDS-ON TIME** 30 MIN.   **TOTAL TIME** 30 MIN.

1   lb. skinned and boned chicken breasts, cut into thin strips

½   tsp. table salt

¼   cup cornstarch

4   Tbsp. vegetable oil, divided

½   lb. Broccolini or fresh green beans, cut into 1-inch pieces

1   cup chicken broth, divided

1   red bell pepper, cut into thin strips

1   small yellow squash, thinly sliced into half moons

¼   cup sliced green onions

2   tsp. cornstarch

1   Tbsp. fresh lime juice

1½   tsp. soy sauce

1   tsp. Asian chili-garlic sauce

Hot cooked rice

Garnish: fresh cilantro

1. Sprinkle chicken with salt; toss with ¼ cup cornstarch.

2. Stir-fry chicken in 3 Tbsp. hot oil in a large skillet or wok over medium-high heat 5 to 6 minutes or until golden brown and done. Transfer to a plate, using a slotted spoon; keep warm. Add Broccolini and ¼ cup broth to skillet; cover and cook 1 to 2 minutes or until crisp-tender. Transfer to plate with chicken, using slotted spoon.

3. Add remaining 1 Tbsp. oil to skillet. Sauté bell pepper and next 2 ingredients in hot oil 2 minutes or until crisp-tender.

4. Whisk together 2 tsp. cornstarch and remaining ¾ cup broth until cornstarch dissolves. Add broth mixture, chicken, and Broccolini (with any accumulated juices) to bell pepper mixture in skillet. Cook, stirring often, 1 minute or until liquid thickens. Stir in lime juice and next 2 ingredients. Serve over hot cooked rice.

QUICK TIP Broccolini is now widely available and is a welcome new vegetable to try, but fresh green beans are a great alternative.

make ahead

Cut, slice, and chop all the vegetables and chicken the night before so you can just throw them into the skillet for a quick dinner.

Basil-Peach Chicken Breasts

MAKES 4 SERVINGS   **HANDS-ON TIME** 30 MIN.   **TOTAL TIME** 45 MIN.

4 skinned and boned chicken breasts (about 2 lb.)

1¼ tsp. kosher salt

½ tsp. freshly ground pepper

2 Tbsp. canola oil

1 shallot, thinly sliced

1 tsp. freshly grated ginger

2 garlic cloves, minced

12 fresh basil leaves, finely chopped

1 cup reduced-sodium fat-free chicken broth

4 large peaches, peeled and cut into ¼-inch-thick slices (about 2 cups)

Garnish: fresh basil leaves

1. Preheat oven to 350°. Season chicken on both sides with salt and pepper. Cook chicken in hot oil in a large ovenproof skillet over medium-high heat 2 minutes on each side or until browned. Remove chicken from skillet, reserving drippings in skillet.

2. Reduce heat to medium. Add shallot to hot drippings in skillet, and sauté 3 minutes or until tender. Add ginger and garlic; sauté 45 to 60 seconds or until fragrant. Add basil, broth, and peaches. Return chicken to skillet, and turn to coat.

3. Bake at 350° for 15 minutes or until chicken is done.

QUICK TIP Starting the chicken on the stovetop and finishing in the oven helps prevent dry, overcooked chicken.

easy side

▶ **Lemon Quinoa:**
Bring 4 cups water, 1½ cups uncooked quinoa, 1 tsp. lemon zest, 1 Tbsp. fresh lemon juice, and ½ tsp. kosher salt to a boil in large saucepan over high heat. Cover, reduce heat to medium-low, and simmer 8 to 10 minutes or until tender; drain. Return to saucepan; cover. Let stand 10 minutes; fluff with a fork before serving.

Chicken Marsala

MAKES 4 SERVINGS   **HANDS-ON TIME** 40 MIN.   **TOTAL TIME** 45 MIN.

- ⅓ cup all-purpose flour
- 1 cup toasted pecan pieces, divided
- 4 skinned and boned chicken breasts (about 1½ lb.)
- 1 tsp. table salt
- ½ tsp. pepper
- 2 Tbsp. butter
- 2 Tbsp. olive oil
- 8 oz. assorted mushrooms, trimmed and sliced
- 2 shallots, sliced
- ¾ cup chicken broth
- ½ cup Marsala
- ¼ cup coarsely chopped fresh flat-leaf parsley

1. Process flour and ⅓ cup pecans in a food processor until finely ground; place flour mixture in a large shallow bowl.

2. Place chicken between 2 sheets of heavy-duty plastic wrap; flatten to ¼-inch thickness, using a rolling pin or flat side of a meat mallet. Sprinkle chicken with salt and pepper; lightly dredge in flour mixture.

3. Melt butter with olive oil in a large nonstick skillet over medium-high heat; add chicken, and cook 2 to 3 minutes on each side or until golden brown and done. Remove chicken from skillet.

4. Add mushrooms and shallots to skillet; sauté 3 minutes or until mushrooms are tender. Add broth and Marsala to skillet, stirring to loosen particles from bottom of skillet. Bring mixture to a boil, reduce heat to medium, and cook, stirring occasionally, 5 minutes or until sauce is slightly thickened. Return chicken to skillet, and cook 1 to 2 minutes or until thoroughly heated.

5. Transfer chicken to a serving platter; spoon mushroom-Marsala mixture over chicken, and sprinkle with parsley and remaining ⅔ cup toasted pecans.

QUICK TIP Marsala is a fortified wine with a smoky flavor that ranges from dry to sweet. Choose a dry Marsala for this recipe.

easy side

Roasted Sweet Potatoes: Preheat oven to 425°. Cube 2 large sweet potatoes (about 2 lb.), and toss with 2 Tbsp. olive oil. Bake for 25 minutes. Remove from oven, and toss with 1 tsp. table salt and ½ tsp. pepper.

Smoky Chicken Barbecue Kabobs

MAKES 8 SERVINGS   **HANDS-ON TIME** 20 MIN.
TOTAL TIME 30 MIN., INCLUDING WHITE BARBECUE SAUCE

- 2 lb. skinned and boned chicken breasts
- ½ large red onion, cut into fourths and separated into pieces
- 1 pt. cherry tomatoes
- 8 (8-inch) metal skewers
- 2 Tbsp. firmly packed dark brown sugar
- 2 tsp. garlic salt
- 1 tsp. chipotle chili powder
- ½ tsp. ground cumin
- ¼ tsp. dried oregano
- White Barbecue Sauce

1. Preheat grill to 350° to 400° (medium-high) heat. Cut chicken into 1-inch cubes. Thread chicken, onion, and tomatoes alternately onto skewers, leaving a ¼-inch space between pieces.

2. Stir together brown sugar and next 4 ingredients. Sprinkle kabobs with brown sugar mixture. Grill kabobs, covered with grill lid, 4 to 5 minutes on each side. Serve with White Barbecue Sauce.

White Barbecue Sauce

MAKES 1¾ CUPS   **HANDS-ON TIME** 5 MIN.   **TOTAL TIME** 5 MIN.

- 1½ cups mayonnaise
- ⅓ cup white vinegar
- 1 tsp. pepper
- ½ tsp. table salt
- ½ tsp. sugar
- 1 garlic clove, pressed

Stir together all ingredients in a small bowl.

QUICK TIP To ensure kabobs won't stick to grill grates, coat grates with cooking spray before heating grill.

easy side

▶ **Vinegar Slaw:** Whisk together 1 Tbsp. sugar, 3 Tbsp. cider vinegar, 2 tsp. vegetable oil, and ¼ tsp. table salt in a large bowl until sugar dissolves. Add 1 (16-oz.) package coleslaw mix and ¼ cup chopped green onion to vinegar mixture; toss until well coated. Serve immediately.

make ahead

▶ You can prepare the White Barbecue Sauce a few days in advance. Just keep chilled until ready to serve.

Chicken Cutlets with Pecan Sauce

MAKES 4 SERVINGS   **HANDS-ON TIME** 23 MIN.   **TOTAL TIME** 23 MIN.

¼ cup butter, divided

½ cup chopped pecans

4 chicken cutlets (about 1¼ lb.)

1 tsp. table salt

½ tsp. pepper

3 Tbsp. all-purpose flour

3 Tbsp. olive oil

½ cup chicken broth

1 Tbsp. brown sugar

2 Tbsp. apple cider vinegar

½ tsp. dried thyme

1. Melt 2 Tbsp. butter in a large nonstick skillet over medium-low heat, and cook pecans, stirring often, 2 to 3 minutes or until toasted and fragrant. Remove from skillet.

2. Sprinkle chicken with salt and pepper. Dredge in flour.

3. Cook chicken in hot oil in skillet over medium heat 3 to 4 minutes on each side or until golden brown and done. Transfer to a serving platter. Top with toasted pecans.

4. Add chicken broth to skillet, and cook 2 minutes, stirring to loosen particles from bottom of skillet. Add brown sugar, vinegar, and thyme, and cook 3 to 4 minutes or until sugar is melted and sauce is slightly thickened. Whisk in remaining 2 Tbsp. butter. Serve sauce over chicken.

QUICK TIP You can use 1½ tsp. chopped fresh thyme in this recipe instead of dried thyme, if you prefer.

easy side

Steamed Vegetables: Prepare 1 (11-oz.) package frozen steam-in-bag baby mixed vegetables according to package directions. Toss with 1 tsp. freshly ground garlic-pepper seasoning. We tested with Green Giant Valley Fresh Steamers Market Blend and McCormick seasoning.

Grilled Chicken and New Potatoes

MAKES 4 SERVINGS   **HANDS-ON TIME** 20 MIN.   **TOTAL TIME** 30 MIN.

Cut leeks in half lengthwise; rinse under running water, separating the layers and rubbing the leaves to remove dirt.

- 1   medium leek, cleaned and thinly sliced
- 1½ lb. small new potatoes, halved
- 2   Tbsp. bell pepper-and-garlic seasoning, divided
- 4   Tbsp. olive oil, divided
- 1½ tsp. table salt, divided
- 1½ lb. chicken breast tenders
- 2   Tbsp. fresh lemon juice, divided
- 2   bunches green onions

1. Preheat grill to 350° to 400° (medium-high) heat.

2. Toss together leek, potatoes, 1 Tbsp. garlic seasoning, 3 Tbsp. olive oil, and 1 tsp. salt.

3. Divide leek mixture among 2 large pieces of heavy-duty aluminum foil. Bring foil sides up over mixture; double fold top and sides to seal, making packets.

4. Grill foil packets, covered with grill lid, 12 minutes.

5. Meanwhile, toss together chicken, 1 Tbsp. lemon juice, remaining 1 Tbsp. garlic seasoning, 1 Tbsp. olive oil, and ½ tsp. salt.

6. Shake foil packets, using tongs, and return to grill. At the same time, grill chicken, covered with grill lid, 5 minutes; turn chicken. Place green onions on grill, and grill chicken, onions, and foil packets 4 to 5 minutes or until chicken is done.

7. Open foil packets carefully, using tongs. Arrange grilled vegetables, chicken, and green onions on a serving plate. Drizzle with remaining 1 Tbsp. lemon juice.

Note: We tested with McCormick Perfect Pinch Roasted Garlic & Bell Pepper Seasoning.

> **QUICK TIP** Use a foil packet as a fuss-free cooking vessel for the leeks and potatoes (or any vegetable).

easy side

▸ **Peach Sangria:**
Combine 1 (750-ml.) bottle rosé wine, ¾ cup vodka, ½ cup peach nectar, 6 Tbsp. frozen lemonade concentrate, and 2 Tbsp. sugar in a pitcher; stir until sugar is dissolved. Stir in 1 lb. sliced, ripe peaches and 1 cup fresh raspberries. Cover and chill 8 hours. Stir in 2 cups chilled club soda just before serving.

Baked Chicken Roulade

MAKES 4 SERVINGS **HANDS-ON TIME** 30 MIN. **TOTAL TIME** 45 MIN.

 4 skinned and boned chicken breasts (about 1½ lb.), pounded thin

 ½ tsp. pepper

 ¼ tsp. table salt

 1 (5-oz.) package baby spinach

 4 garlic cloves, minced and divided

 2 tsp. olive oil

 12 fresh thin asparagus spears (about 1 lb.)

 Wooden picks

 5 Tbsp. butter, divided

 2 Tbsp. olive oil

 1 Tbsp. all-purpose flour

 2 Tbsp. dry white wine

 ¾ cup chicken broth

 1 tsp. fresh lemon juice

 2 Tbsp. chopped fresh flat-leaf parsley

 2 Tbsp. drained capers

1. Preheat oven to 425°. Sprinkle chicken with pepper and salt. Sauté spinach and 2 garlic cloves in 2 tsp. hot oil in large ovenproof skillet over medium heat 1 minute or until spinach begins to wilt. Transfer spinach mixture to a plate. Wipe skillet clean.

2. Spoon spinach mixture over each breast, leaving a ½-inch border around edges. Top with asparagus, and roll up, starting at 1 short side. Tuck in ends of chicken, and secure with wooden picks.

3. Melt 3 Tbsp. butter with 2 Tbsp. olive oil in skillet over medium-high heat; add chicken. Cook 6 to 8 minutes, turning to brown on all sides. Transfer skillet to oven, and bake at 425° for 15 minutes. Transfer to a serving plate, and cover with aluminum foil to keep warm.

4. Melt remaining 2 Tbsp. butter in skillet over medium-high heat; add remaining garlic. Sauté 1 to 2 minutes or until tender and fragrant. Whisk in flour; cook 1 minute. Add white wine; cook, stirring constantly, 1 minute. Whisk in chicken broth and lemon juice; cook 2 minutes or until thickened. Stir in parsley and capers; spoon sauce over chicken.

QUICK TIP To flatten, place chicken breasts between sheets of heavy-duty plastic wrap and pound with a mallet or rolling pin.

easy side

Roasted Potatoes:
Preheat oven to 450°. Stir together 3 lb. quartered baby red potatoes, 1 Tbsp. peanut oil, and 1 tsp. kosher salt in a large bowl. Place potatoes in a single layer in a lightly greased 15- x 10-inch jelly-roll pan. Bake 40 to 45 minutes or until tender and browned, stirring twice. Garnish with fresh rosemary.

Versatile and flavorful, pork chops and tenderloins are not only a great source of lean protein, but they are a great way to stretch your dollar.

GRILLED PORK CHOPS WITH PEACH AGRODOLCE, PAGE 192 ▶

Spicy Pork-and-Orange Chopped Salad

MAKES 4 SERVINGS   **HANDS-ON TIME** 28 MIN.   **TOTAL TIME** 33 MIN.

Combining romaine, coleslaw mix, cucumber, and almonds makes this dish crispy and crunchy.

- 1   lb. pork tenderloin, cut into ½-inch pieces
- 2½ tsp. Asian seasoning blend
- ½   tsp. table salt
- 1   Tbsp. olive oil
- 2   oranges
- ½   cup bottled low-fat sesame-ginger dressing
- 1   cup seeded and chopped cucumber
- ¼   cup chopped fresh cilantro
- 1   romaine lettuce heart, chopped
- 3   cups shredded coleslaw mix
- ½   cup wasabi-and-soy sauce-flavored almonds
- **Garnish: orange slices**

1. Toss pork with Asian seasoning and salt to coat. Sauté pork in hot oil in a large nonstick skillet over medium-high heat 8 to 10 minutes or until done.

2. Peel oranges, and cut into ½-inch-thick slices. Cut slices into chunks.

3. Pour dressing into a salad bowl. Stir in oranges, cucumber, and cilantro. Let stand 5 minutes. Add romaine, coleslaw mix, and pork; toss gently. Sprinkle with almonds. Serve immediately.

Note: We tested with McCormick Perfect Pinch Asian Seasoning and Blue Diamond Bold Wasabi & Soy Sauce Almonds.

QUICK TIP Look for wasabi-and-soy sauce-flavored almonds in cans sold alongside cocktail peanuts.

easy side

Toasted Cheese Baguettes: Preheat oven to 425°. Spread a thin layer of butter onto 1 side of 12 (½-inch-thick) French bread baguette slices. Bake 4 minutes or until toasted. Combine 2 Tbsp. mayonnaise with 1 cup (4 oz.) grated extra-sharp Cheddar cheese. Spread onto 1 side of bread. Bake 5 to 6 minutes or until cheese is melted.

Molasses-Balsamic Pork Kabobs with Green Tomatoes and Plums

MAKES 4 TO 6 SERVINGS   **HANDS-ON TIME** 20 MIN.
TOTAL TIME 1 HOUR, 8 MIN.

- 8 (12-inch) wooden or metal skewers
- 1 (1.5-lb.) package pork tenderloin, trimmed and cut into 1½-inch pieces
- 4 large plums, quartered
- 2 medium-size green tomatoes, cut into eighths
- 2 medium-size red onions, cut into eighths
- 2 tsp. seasoned salt
- 2 tsp. pepper
- ½ cup molasses
- ¼ cup balsamic vinegar

1. Soak wooden skewers in water 30 minutes.

2. Preheat grill to 350° to 400° (medium-high). Thread pork and next 3 ingredients alternately onto skewers, leaving ¼ inch between pieces. Sprinkle kabobs with seasoned salt and pepper. Stir together molasses and vinegar.

3. Grill kabobs, covered with grill lid, for 12 minutes, turning after 6 minutes. Baste kabobs with half of molasses mixture, and grill 3 more minutes. Turn kabobs, baste with remaining half of molasses mixture, and grill 3 more minutes or until done.

QUICK TIP Soaking wooden skewers is an important step in this recipe to ensure they don't burn on the grill. Don't skip it!

easy side

Garlic Rice with Cilantro and Corn: Prepare 2 (8.5-oz.) packages ready-to-serve roasted garlic whole grain rice according to package directions. Stir in 1 (8-oz.) can sweet white kernel corn, drained, and ¼ cup chopped fresh cilantro.

Pork Fried Rice

MAKES 6 SERVINGS **HANDS-ON TIME** 30 MIN. **TOTAL TIME** 30 MIN.

- 1 lb. boneless pork chops, cut into strips
- ½ tsp. pepper
- 1 Tbsp. sesame oil, divided
- ¾ cup diced carrots
- ½ cup chopped onion
- 3 green onions, chopped
- 1 Tbsp. butter
- 2 large eggs, lightly beaten
- 2 cups cooked long-grain white or jasmine rice, chilled
- ½ cup frozen English peas, thawed (optional)
- ¼ cup soy sauce

1. Season pork with pepper. Cook pork in 1½ tsp. hot oil in a large skillet over medium heat 7 to 8 minutes or until done. Remove pork from skillet.

2. Heat remaining 1½ tsp. oil in skillet; sauté carrots and onion in hot oil 2 to 3 minutes or until tender. Stir in green onions, and sauté 1 minute. Remove mixture from skillet. Wipe skillet clean.

3. Melt butter in skillet. Add eggs to skillet, and cook, without stirring, 1 minute or until eggs begin to set on bottom. Gently draw cooked edges away from sides of pan to form large pieces. Cook, stirring occasionally, 30 seconds to 1 minute or until thickened and moist. (Do not overstir.) Add pork, carrot mixture, rice, and, if desired, peas to skillet; cook over medium heat, stirring often, 2 to 3 minutes or until thoroughly heated. Stir in soy sauce. Serve immediately.

Note: Use leftover rice, or prepare 1 (8-oz.) pouch ready-to-serve jasmine rice according to package directions, and chill.

> **QUICK TIP** Chilling rice will help keep it from clumping while stir-frying.

easy side

Sesame-Ginger Cucumbers: Stir together 1 English cucumber, thinly sliced into half moons; 3 Tbsp. bottled sesame-ginger vinaigrette; 1 Tbsp. chopped fresh cilantro; and 1 tsp. toasted sesame seeds. Cover and chill until ready to serve.

Cumin-Crusted Pork Cutlets

MAKES 4 TO 6 SERVINGS   **HANDS-ON TIME** 27 MIN.   **TOTAL TIME** 27 MIN.

- 3 whole-wheat bread slices
- 2 Tbsp. self-rising yellow cornmeal mix
- ½ tsp. ground cumin
- 8 thinly sliced boneless pork loin chops (about 1¼ lb.)
- ½ tsp. table salt
- ¼ tsp. pepper
- 1 large egg
- 2 Tbsp. whole grain mustard
- ¼ cup olive oil

1. Process bread in a food processor until finely crumbled. Combine breadcrumbs, cornmeal mix, and cumin in a shallow bowl.

2. Sprinkle pork chops with salt and pepper. Whisk together egg, mustard, and 2 Tbsp. water until blended. Dip pork in egg mixture; dredge in breadcrumb mixture, pressing to adhere.

3. Cook half of pork in 2 Tbsp. hot oil in a large nonstick skillet over medium heat 3 to 4 minutes on each side or until golden brown. Keep warm in a 200° oven. Repeat procedure with remaining pork and oil. Serve warm.

QUICK TIP Whole-wheat bread is great for breadcrumbs because it packs more flavor and crumbles easily in a food processor.

easy side

Cabbage-and-Apple Slaw:
Sauté 4 cups shredded red cabbage, 1 cup thinly sliced sweet onion, and 1 thinly sliced Granny Smith apple in 2 Tbsp. hot olive oil until tender. Add 2 Tbsp. each red wine vinegar and brown sugar, and cook until sugar is dissolved. Sprinkle with salt and pepper to taste.

Sage-and-Pecan Pork Tenderloin Cutlets

MAKES 4 SERVINGS   **HANDS-ON TIME** 35 MIN.   **TOTAL TIME** 51 MIN.

If you love fried pork chops, try this recipe. Pork cutlets are low in fat, and this recipe is "fried" with just enough heart-healthy oil for the crispy crunch you crave.

- 1 cup red wine vinegar
- 5 Tbsp. seedless blackberry preserves
- ½ tsp. table salt
- ¾ cup fine, dry breadcrumbs
- ½ cup finely chopped pecans
- 2 tsp. rubbed sage
- 1 lb. pork cutlets
- 2 large eggs, beaten
- 4 tsp. olive oil

Garnishes: fresh blackberries, fresh sage leaves

1. Bring vinegar to a boil in a small saucepan over medium-high heat. Reduce heat to medium, and cook 6 minutes or until reduced by half. Stir in preserves, and cook 5 minutes. Stir in salt.

2. Stir together breadcrumbs, pecans, and sage in a shallow bowl.

3. Dredge pork in breadcrumb mixture, dip in beaten eggs, and dredge again in breadcrumb mixture.

4. Cook half of pork cutlets in 2 tsp. hot oil in a large nonstick skillet over medium heat 8 minutes or until done, turning every 2 minutes. Repeat procedure with remaining pork and oil. Serve with blackberry vinegar sauce.

QUICK TIP Make cutlets by slicing a 1-lb. pork tenderloin into 8 slices and pounding with a mallet to ¼-inch thickness.

easy side

Mango Garden Salad: Toss together 4 cups arugula; ½ English cucumber, thinly sliced; 1 cup cherry tomatoes, halved; 1 mango, chopped; and ½ red onion, thinly sliced in a large bowl. Drizzle with bottled red wine vinaigrette.

make ahead

You can prepare blackberry vinegar sauce up to one day ahead. Keep chilled, and warm sauce before serving.

Grilled Pork Tenderloin with Squash Medley

MAKES 4 SERVINGS   **HANDS-ON TIME** 10 MIN.   **TOTAL TIME** 50 MIN.

- 1 (1-lb.) pork tenderloin
- 2 tsp. table salt, divided
- ¾ tsp. pepper, divided
- 2 Tbsp. Dijon mustard
- 1 Tbsp. chopped fresh thyme
- 1 Tbsp. olive oil
- 1 Tbsp. honey
- 1 garlic clove, minced
- 2 yellow squash
- 2 zucchini
- 1 tsp. olive oil
- 1 tsp. fresh thyme leaves

1. Preheat grill to 350° to 400° (medium-high) heat. Remove silver skin from tenderloin, leaving a thin layer of fat.

2. Sprinkle pork with 1 tsp. salt and ½ tsp. pepper. Combine mustard and next 4 ingredients. Rub mustard mixture on pork; cover and let stand 10 minutes.

3. Preheat oven to 450°. Cut squash and zucchini into ½-inch slices; cut into half moons. Toss with 1 tsp. olive oil and remaining 1 tsp. salt and ¼ tsp. pepper. Place on an aluminum foil-lined jelly-roll pan, and bake at 450° for 20 minutes or until tender.

4. Meanwhile, grill pork, covered with grill lid, 10 to 12 minutes on each side or until a meat thermometer inserted into thickest portion registers 155°. Remove from grill; cover with foil, and let stand 10 minutes. Slice pork, and serve with squash medley. Sprinkle with thyme.

QUICK TIP Allowing the grilled pork to rest before slicing is the best way to ensure juicy, flavorful results.

easy side

Creamy Mashed Potatoes: Prepare 1 (24-oz.) package frozen steam-and-mash potatoes according to package directions. Stir in ⅓ cup whipped chive-flavored cream cheese. Add pepper to taste and 2 Tbsp. melted butter.

Bourbon-Brown Sugar Pork Tenderloin

MAKES 6 TO 8 SERVINGS   **HANDS-ON TIME** 30 MIN.
TOTAL TIME 8 HOURS, 46 MIN.

It's a fresh, weeknight-easy spin on Sunday pork roast with gravy. A quick reduction transforms the flavorful marinade into an indulgent sauce.

2 (1-lb.) pork tenderloins

¼ cup firmly packed dark brown sugar

¼ cup minced green onions

¼ cup bourbon

¼ cup soy sauce

¼ cup Dijon mustard

½ tsp. freshly ground pepper

½ tsp. cornstarch

1. Remove silver skin from tenderloins, leaving a thin layer of fat. Combine brown sugar and next 5 ingredients in a large zip-top plastic freezer bag; add pork. Seal bag, and chill 8 to 18 hours, turning bag occasionally. Remove pork from marinade, reserving marinade.

2. Preheat grill to 350° to 400° (medium-high) heat. Grill pork, covered with grill lid, 8 minutes on each side or until a meat thermometer inserted into thickest portion registers 155°. Remove from grill, and let stand 10 minutes.

3. Meanwhile, combine reserved marinade and cornstarch in a saucepan. Bring to a boil over medium heat; cook, stirring constantly, 1 minute. Cut pork diagonally into thin slices, and arrange on a serving platter; drizzle with warm sauce.

QUICK TIP Using the marinade as a sauce adds more flavor to the pork; just be sure it comes to a full boil in Step 3.

easy side

Orange-Spice Sweet Potatoes: Preheat oven to 400°. Bake 3 lb. sweet potatoes 1 hour or until tender; peel. Beat potatoes, ½ cup packed brown sugar, ⅓ cup orange juice, 1 tsp. ground cinnamon, 1 tsp. orange zest, ¼ tsp. ground nutmeg, and ¼ tsp. ground ginger in a large bowl at medium speed with an electric mixer until smooth. Cover and microwave on HIGH 1 to 2 minutes or until heated through.

Spicy Grilled Pork Tenderloin with Blackberry Sauce

MAKES 6 TO 8 SERVINGS   **HANDS-ON TIME** 15 MIN.   **TOTAL TIME** 35 MIN.

- 2 (¾-lb.) pork tenderloins
- 1 Tbsp. olive oil
- 1½ Tbsp. Caribbean jerk seasoning
- 1 tsp. table salt
- ⅔ cup seedless blackberry preserves
- ¼ cup Dijon mustard
- 2 Tbsp. rum or orange juice
- 1 Tbsp. orange zest
- 1 Tbsp. grated fresh ginger

1. Preheat grill to 350° to 400° (medium-high) heat. Remove silver skin from tenderloins, leaving a thin layer of fat. Brush tenderloins with oil, and rub with seasoning and salt.

2. Grill tenderloins, covered with grill lid, 10 minutes on each side or until a meat thermometer inserted into thickest portion registers 155°. Remove from grill, and let stand 10 minutes.

3. Meanwhile, whisk together blackberry preserves and next 4 ingredients in a small saucepan, and cook over low heat, whisking constantly, 5 minutes or until thoroughly heated.

4. Cut pork diagonally into thin slices, and arrange on a serving platter; drizzle with warm sauce.

QUICK TIP To save time, ask your butcher to remove the silver skin from tenderloins.

easy side

Tropical Salad: In a large bowl, whisk together ¼ cup olive oil, ¼ cup fresh lemon juice, 1 Tbsp. white balsamic vinegar, 1 minced garlic clove, 1 tsp. sugar, ½ tsp. table salt, and ¼ tsp. pepper until blended. Add 1 (5-oz.) container fresh arugula, 1 chopped mango, and 1 cup blackberries; toss to coat.

Roasted Pork with Dried Fruit and Port Sauce

MAKES 8 SERVINGS   **HANDS-ON TIME** 25 MIN.   **TOTAL TIME** 49 MIN.

- 2 (1-lb.) pork tenderloins
- 1 tsp. table salt
- ½ tsp. pepper
- 7 tsp. olive oil, divided
- 1 cup dried apricots
- 1 cup dried pitted plums
- 1 cup dried peaches
- ½ cup dried tart cherries
- ¼ cup pine nuts
- 1 cup port wine
- 1 cup pomegranate juice
- 2 (2½-inch) cinnamon sticks
- ½ cup chicken broth

1. Preheat oven to 425°. Remove silver skin from tenderloins, leaving a thin layer of fat. Sprinkle pork with salt and pepper. Cook pork in 6 tsp. hot oil in a large skillet over medium-high heat 3 minutes on each side or until golden brown. Transfer pork to a lightly greased jelly-roll or roasting pan, reserving drippings in skillet.

2. Bake at 425° for 18 to 20 minutes or until a meat thermometer inserted into thickest portion registers 155°. Remove from oven; cover and let stand 10 minutes or until thermometer registers 155°.

3. Meanwhile, add remaining 1 tsp. oil to hot drippings in skillet. Add apricots and next 4 ingredients, and sauté over medium-high heat 3 minutes or until pine nuts are toasted and fragrant. Add port wine and next 2 ingredients. Bring to a boil; reduce heat to low, and simmer 5 minutes or until mixture slightly thickens. Stir in broth, and simmer 15 minutes or until fruit is tender. Serve with sliced pork.

QUICK TIP A mixture of dried fruit makes this pork special. Other options include raisins, dried cranberries, and dried apples.

easy side

Green Bean-and-Red Bell Pepper Toss: Melt 2 Tbsp. butter in a large Dutch oven over medium-high heat. Add 2 (8-oz.) packages French green beans; 1 red bell pepper, cut into strips; 3 sliced shallots; 2 minced garlic cloves, ½ tsp. table salt, and ⅛ tsp. ground red pepper, tossing to coat. Add ¼ cup water. Cook, covered, 4 to 6 minutes; uncover and cook, stirring often, 1 to 2 more minutes or until water is evaporated and beans are crisp-tender.

Peach-Mustard-Glazed Pork Tenderloin

MAKES 8 SERVINGS   **HANDS-ON TIME** 30 MIN.   **TOTAL TIME** 1 HOUR

- 2 (1-lb.) pork tenderloins
- ½ tsp. table salt
- ½ tsp. freshly ground black pepper
- 2 Tbsp. olive oil
- 2 Tbsp. butter
- 1 large shallot, minced
- ½ cup peach preserves
- ⅓ cup bourbon
- 2 Tbsp. country-style Dijon mustard
- ¼ tsp. dried crushed red pepper
- ½ cup reduced-sodium chicken broth

1. Preheat oven to 400°. Remove silver skin from tenderloins, leaving a layer of fat. Sprinkle tenderloins with salt and pepper. Cook in hot oil in a large ovenproof skillet over high heat 3 to 4 minutes on each side or until lightly browned.

2. Melt butter in a small skillet over medium-high heat; add shallot, and sauté 2 to 3 minutes until tender. Remove from heat, and stir in peach preserves and next 3 ingredients. Cook over medium heat, stirring often, 1 minute or until preserves are melted. Pour over tenderloins.

3. Bake at 400° for 20 minutes or until a meat thermometer inserted in thickest portion registers 155°. Transfer to a cutting board, reserving drippings in skillet. Cover loosely with aluminum foil, and let stand 10 minutes before slicing.

4. Meanwhile, stir broth into reserved drippings, and cook over medium-high heat, stirring constantly, 5 minutes or until reduced by half. Serve with sliced tenderloins.

QUICK TIP Bourbon adds intense flavor to the peach-mustard sauce; however, chicken broth can be substituted.

easy side

Spicy Broccoli Rabe:
Bring 8 cups of water to a boil in a large saucepan. Cook 1 lb. broccoli rabe, cut into 2-inch pieces, in boiling water 2 minutes; drain. Heat a large nonstick skillet over medium heat. Add 1 Tbsp. olive oil, ⅛ tsp. crushed red pepper, and 3 thinly sliced garlic cloves to pan; cook 30 seconds, stirring occasionally. Add broccoli rabe to pan; cook 2 minutes. Stir in salt and black pepper to taste.

Lemon Pork Chops with Quinoa Salad

MAKES 6 SERVINGS   **HANDS-ON TIME** 30 MIN.
TOTAL TIME 55 MIN., INCLUDING LEMON-GARLIC VINAIGRETTE

- 6 (½-inch-thick) bone-in center-cut pork rib chops (about 4 lb.)
- 2 Tbsp. lemon-herb seasoning
- 1¼ tsp. kosher salt, divided
- 6 Tbsp. olive oil, divided
- 1 (8-oz.) package fresh sugar snap peas
- 1 garlic clove, sliced
- 3 cups cooked quinoa
- Lemon-Garlic Vinaigrette
- ⅓ cup loosely packed fresh flat-leaf parsley leaves
- ¼ cup chopped dry-roasted almonds

1. Rub pork chops with herb seasoning and 1 tsp. kosher salt. Sear half of pork in 2 ½ Tbsp. hot olive oil in a large skillet over medium-high heat 4 to 5 minutes on each side or until browned. Repeat procedure with 2½ Tbsp. olive oil and remaining pork.

2. Cut sugar snap peas in half crosswise. Heat remaining 1 Tbsp. olive oil in skillet over medium-high heat; cook peas in hot oil 1 minute or until bright green and tender. Sprinkle with remaining ¼ tsp. kosher salt. Add garlic; sauté 1 minute. Remove from heat.

3. Add quinoa and Lemon-Garlic Vinaigrette to sugar snap pea mixture, and toss to coat. Stir in parsley and almonds. Serve with pork.

Lemon-Garlic Vinaigrette

MAKES ¼ CUP   **HANDS-ON TIME** 5 MIN.   **TOTAL TIME** 5 MIN.

Whisk together 2 Tbsp. lemon juice, 1 Tbsp. olive oil, 2 minced garlic cloves, ¼ tsp. kosher salt, and ¼ tsp. pepper.

QUICK TIP Quinoa is a protein-packed grain alternative to rice or couscous; 1½ cups uncooked equals 3 cups cooked.

easy side

Goat Cheese Crostini: Stir together 2 oz. softened goat cheese, ½ tsp. chopped fresh oregano, ½ tsp. chopped fresh thyme, and ¼ tsp. freshly ground pepper in a small bowl. Spread goat cheese mixture on 8 toasted ½-inch-thick diagonally cut French bread baguette slices.

Grilled Pork Chops with Peach Agrodolce

MAKES 4 SERVINGS   **HANDS-ON TIME** 15 MIN.
TOTAL TIME 1 HOUR, 25 MIN., INCLUDING PEACH AGRODOLCE

- 4 (1½-inch-thick) pork porterhouse chops (about 2½ lb.)
- 1 Tbsp. olive oil
- ¾ tsp. kosher salt
- ½ tsp. freshly ground pepper
- Peach Agrodolce

1. Let pork stand at room temperature 30 minutes. Prepare 1 side of grill, heating to 350° to 400° (medium-high) heat; leave other side unlit. Brush pork with olive oil, and sprinkle with salt and pepper.

2. Grill pork over lit side of grill, covered with grill lid, 4 minutes on each side; transfer pork to unlit side, and grill, covered with grill lid, 10 minutes on each side or until a meat thermometer registers 155°. Let stand 5 minutes. Arrange pork on a serving platter, and top with Peach Agrodolce.

Peach Agrodolce

MAKES 1½ CUPS   **HANDS-ON TIME** 15 MIN.   **TOTAL TIME** 15 MIN.

- 2 Tbsp. raisins
- 2 Tbsp. tawny port wine
- 1 Tbsp. chopped fresh parsley
- 1 Tbsp. balsamic vinegar
- 1 Tbsp. olive oil
- 2 large fresh, ripe peaches, peeled and chopped

Cook raisins, port, and 2 Tbsp. water in a small saucepan over medium heat, stirring occasionally, 5 minutes. Remove from heat; whisk in parsley, vinegar, and oil. Stir in peaches and salt and pepper to taste.

QUICK TIP Heating only one side of the grill allows you to sear the chops first, then cook them over indirect heat slowly until done.

make ahead

You can prepare Peach Agrodolce up to 4 hours ahead. Keep chilled and let sit at room temperature 30 minutes before serving.

8 GROUND MEAT

Ground chicken, beef, and turkey are for more than just making burgers! Try a meaty chili, a hearty casserole, or a loaded tostada for delicious weeknight suppers.

TURKEY CHILI PAGE 206 ▶

Grilled Chicken Tequila Burgers

MAKES 5 SERVINGS   **HANDS-ON TIME** 15 MIN.   **TOTAL TIME** 35 MIN.

- 1 lb. ground chicken breast
- 4 Tbsp. chopped fresh cilantro, divided
- 2 chopped garlic cloves
- 1 seeded and chopped jalapeño pepper
- ½ cup panko (Japanese breadcrumbs) or ¼ cup uncooked regular or quick-cooking oats
- 2 Tbsp. tequila
- ¾ tsp. table salt
- ½ tsp. pepper
- ¼ tsp. soy sauce
- 2 tsp. lime zest, divided
- 1 bell pepper, sliced
- 1 medium onion, sliced
- ¾ cup mayonnaise
- 1 tsp. chopped fresh chives
- 1 tsp. fresh lime juice
- 5 hamburger buns

1. Preheat grill to 350° to 400° (medium-high) heat. Pulse ground chicken, 3 Tbsp. cilantro, garlic, and jalapeño pepper in a food processor 3 to 4 times or until combined. Add panko or oats, next 4 ingredients, and 1 tsp. lime zest; pulse until combined. Shape into 5 patties.

2. Grill, covered with grill lid, 4 to 5 minutes on each side or until a meat thermometer inserted in thickest portion registers 165°; remove from grill. Keep warm. Reduce grill temperature to 300° to 350° (medium) heat. Grill sliced bell peppers and onions 4 minutes on each side or until tender. Stir together mayonnaise, 1 Tbsp. cilantro, chives, 1 tsp. lime zest, and lime juice. Serve burgers, bell pepper slices, and onion slices on buns with mayonnaise mixture.

QUICK TIP If chicken burgers are too soft to handle easily, pop them in the fridge for 15 minutes.

easy side

Buttermilk Onion Rings: Cut 2 large onions into ½-inch slices, and separate into rings. Set aside. Whisk together 2 cups buttermilk and 1¼ cup all-purpose baking mix until smooth. Pour peanut oil to a depth of 2 inches in a Dutch oven; heat to 375°. Dip onion rings in batter, coating well. Fry a few rings at a time, until golden. Drain on paper towels. Serve immediately.

Turkey Burger Patty Melts

MAKES 6 SERVINGS   **HANDS-ON TIME** 45 MIN.   **TOTAL TIME** 45 MIN.

Give patty melts a twist with Thanksgiving flavor!

1½ lb. lean ground turkey

⅔ cup crumbled Gorgonzola cheese

1 tsp. garlic salt

¾ tsp. freshly ground pepper

¾ cup chopped toasted pecans

½ cup canned whole-berry cranberry sauce

⅓ cup Dijon mustard

12 sourdough bread slices

6 (¾-oz.) Monterey Jack cheese slices

3 cups loosely packed fresh arugula

1. Combine ground turkey, next 3 ingredients, and pecans in a large bowl. Shape into 6 (½-inch-thick) patties, shaped to fit bread slices.

2. Cook patties in a large lightly greased skillet over medium heat 5 to 6 minutes on each side or until done.

3. Stir together cranberry sauce and Dijon mustard. Spread 1 Tbsp. cranberry mixture on 1 side of each bread slice. Layer 6 sourdough bread slices with Monterey Jack cheese, arugula, and turkey burgers; top with remaining bread slices, cranberry mixture side down.

4. Cook sandwiches, in 2 batches, on a hot griddle or in a lightly greased skillet over medium heat 2 to 3 minutes on each side or until golden brown and cheese melts.

QUICK TIP Homemade cranberry sauce can be substituted for the canned version, if you have some on hand.

easy side

Creamy Coleslaw:
Combine 1 (16-oz.) package shredded coleslaw mix, 1 (8-oz.) container sour cream, 2 Tbsp. fresh lemon juice, and 1 tsp. salt. Cover and chill until ready to serve.

Pecan-Crusted Pork Burgers

MAKES 4 SERVINGS   **HANDS-ON TIME** 15 MIN.   **TOTAL TIME** 33 MIN.

Vegetable cooking spray

2 apricots, chopped

½ cup mayonnaise

1 canned chipotle chile pepper in adobo sauce, chopped

2 Tbsp. finely chopped green onion

1 Tbsp. adobo sauce from can

1½ lb. lean ground pork

1 Tbsp. butter, melted

½ cup finely chopped pecans

½ tsp. table salt

¼ tsp. black pepper

4 French hamburger buns, split

4 Bibb lettuce leaves

1. Coat cold cooking grate of grill with cooking spray, and place on grill. Preheat grill to 350° to 400°(medium-high) heat. Stir together apricots and next 4 ingredients; set aside.

2. Gently combine pork and 2 Tbsp. mayonnaise mixture until blended, using hands. Shape into 4 (4-inch-wide, 1-inch-thick) patties.

3. Stir together butter and next 3 ingredients in a small bowl until well blended. Sprinkle each patty with about 2 Tbsp. pecan mixture (about 1 Tbsp. on each side), gently pressing to adhere.

4. Grill pecan-covered pork patties, covered with grill lid, 6 to 8 minutes on each side or until a meat thermometer inserted into centers registers 155°.

5. Grill buns, cut sides down, 1 to 2 minutes or until lightly toasted. Serve burgers on buns with lettuce and remaining mayonnaise mixture.

QUICK TIP Ground pork is becoming more and more common in groceries, but you can always ask your butcher to grind it for you.

easy side

Seasoned Curly Fries: Cook 1 (28-oz.) package frozen curly fries according to package directions. Toss with 2 tsp. Cajun seasoning.

Super Simple Sloppy Joes

MAKES 8 SERVINGS   **HANDS-ON TIME** 10 MIN.   **TOTAL TIME** 30 MIN.

If you're looking for a sure-favorite, Sloppy Joes will keep the whole family smiling, and these are just as easy as the version from a can!

1½ lb. lean ground beef
1 (14½-oz.) can diced tomatoes, undrained
1¼ cups ketchup
½ cup bottled barbecue sauce
1 Tbsp. Worcestershire sauce
8 hamburger buns, toasted

1. Cook ground beef in a large skillet over medium-high heat, stirring until it crumbles and is no longer pink; drain well. Return cooked beef to skillet.

2. Stir in tomatoes and next 3 ingredients. Reduce heat to low, and simmer 15 minutes or until thickened. Serve mixture on toasted buns.

QUICK TIP If you like your Sloppy Joes less "sloppy," let the mixture simmer a few more minutes and continue to thicken.

make ahead

Prepare recipe as directed, without buns. Cover and chill Sloppy Joe mixture up to 2 days ahead. Reheat in a skillet over low heat until heated through, and serve on buns.

Tostadas

MAKES 6 SERVINGS   **HANDS-ON TIME** 5 MIN.   **TOTAL TIME** 20 MIN.

Loaded with your favorite toppings, these open-faced tacos make dinner a fiesta!

1½ lb. lean ground beef

1 small onion, chopped

1 package taco seasoning mix

Vegetable oil

6 (8-inch) flour tortillas

1 (15-oz.) can kidney beans, rinsed and drained

1 large tomato, chopped

1 (8-oz.) bag preshredded iceberg lettuce

1 large avocado, peeled and chopped

2 cups (8 oz.) shredded sharp Cheddar cheese

Toppings: sour cream, salsa

1. Cook first 3 ingredients in a large skillet over medium heat, stirring until beef crumbles and is no longer pink; drain and set aside.

2. Pour oil to a depth of ¼ inch in a heavy skillet. Fry tortillas, 1 at a time, in hot oil over high heat 20 seconds on each side or until crisp and golden brown. Drain on paper towels.

3. Layer beef mixture, beans, tomato, and next 3 ingredients on warm tortillas. Serve with desired toppings.

QUICK TIP If you want to make this even easier, skip Step 2 by purchasing tostada shells.

easy side

Cilantro Rice: Heat 2 (10-oz.) packages frozen brown rice according to package directions. Transfer rice to a medium bowl, and stir in ⅔ cup bottled taco sauce and ½ cup chopped fresh cilantro.

make ahead

Fry tortillas up to a day ahead and store in an airtight container at room temperature.

Turkey Chili

MAKES 6 SERVINGS   **HANDS-ON TIME** 15 MIN.   **TOTAL TIME** 50 MIN.

- 1 onion, chopped
- 1 green bell pepper, chopped
- 1 lb. ground turkey
- 1 lb. ground turkey sausage
- 1 tsp. vegetable oil
- 1 (16-oz.) can chili beans
- 2 cups tomato sauce
- 2 cups tomato juice
- 1 garlic clove, minced
- 1 (1.75-oz.) envelope chili seasoning mix
- 1 (10-oz.) can diced tomatoes and green chiles
- 1 tsp. sugar

Garnishes: sour cream, shredded Cheddar cheese

1. Cook onion, bell pepper, ground turkey, and sausage in hot oil in a Dutch oven over medium heat, stirring until meat crumbles and is no longer pink. Drain well.

2. Add chili beans and next 6 ingredients to Dutch oven; bring to a boil, stirring frequently. Reduce heat, and simmer 30 minutes, stirring occasionally.

QUICK TIP The combination of ground turkey and ground turkey sausage gives this chili pumped-up flavor and richness.

make ahead

Prepare recipe as directed, omitting garnishes. Cover and chill up to 2 days ahead. Reheat in a saucepan over low heat.

Baked Linguine with Meat Sauce

MAKES 8 SERVINGS   **HANDS-ON TIME** 40 MIN.
TOTAL TIME 1 HOUR, 15 MIN.

- 2 **lb. lean ground beef**
- 2 **garlic cloves, minced**
- 1 **(28-oz.) can crushed tomatoes**
- 1 **(8-oz.) can tomato sauce**
- 1 **(6-oz.) can tomato paste**
- 2 **tsp. sugar**
- 1 **tsp. table salt**
- 8 **oz. uncooked linguine**
- 1 **(16-oz.) container sour cream**
- 1 **(8-oz.) package cream cheese, softened**
- 1 **bunch green onions, chopped**
- 2 **cups (8 oz.) shredded sharp Cheddar cheese**

1. Preheat oven to 350°. Cook beef and garlic in a Dutch oven, stirring until beef crumbles and is no longer pink. Stir in tomatoes and next 4 ingredients; simmer 30 minutes. Set mixture aside.

2. Cook pasta according to package directions; drain. Place in a lightly greased 13- x 9-inch baking dish.

3. Stir together sour cream, cream cheese, and green onions. Spread over pasta. Top with meat sauce.

4. Bake at 350° for 20 to 25 minutes or until thoroughly heated. Sprinkle with Cheddar cheese, and bake 5 more minutes or until cheese melts. Let stand 5 minutes.

QUICK TIP Be sure to add the cheese just during the last 5 minutes of baking so it's melty and not burned.

easy side

Simple Spinach Salad: Gently toss fresh baby spinach leaves and thinly sliced red onions with bottled balsamic vinaigrette.

make ahead

Prepare recipe as directed through Step 3. Cover and chill up to 1 day ahead. Continue with recipe as directed, baking 10 to 15 more minutes or until thoroughly heated.

Spicy Tomato Meat Sauce with Fettuccine

MAKES 5¼ CUPS   **HANDS-ON TIME** 15 MIN.
TOTAL TIME 1 HOUR, INCLUDING ITALIAN SEASONING MIX

- ½   lb. ground chuck
- 1   Tbsp. extra virgin olive oil
- ½   cup finely chopped onion
- 2   tsp. minced garlic
- 1½   Tbsp. Italian Seasoning Mix
- 1   (28-oz.) can crushed tomatoes
- 1   (8-oz.) can Spanish-style tomato sauce
- 1   tsp. kosher salt
- 1   tsp. honey
- Cooked fettuccine or spaghetti

1. Cook ground chuck in a 3-qt. saucepan over medium heat 6 to 8 minutes until meat crumbles and is no longer pink. Drain; return to pan.

2. Add oil to pan and sauté onion and garlic in hot oil over medium heat 2 to 3 minutes or until tender. Stir in Italian Seasoning Mix, and cook 1 minute. Stir in crushed tomatoes, tomato sauce, and 1 cup water; bring to a boil, stirring constantly.

3. Reduce heat to low, and simmer 40 to 45 minutes or slightly thickened. Stir in salt and honey. Serve over fettuccine.

Italian Seasoning Mix

MAKES: ½ CUP   **HANDS-ON TIME** 5 MIN.   **TOTAL TIME** 5 MIN.

- ½   cup dried basil
- 2   Tbsp. plus 2 tsp. dried oregano
- 4   tsp. dried crushed red pepper
- 2   tsp. whole black peppercorns

Process all ingredients in a food processor 1 minute or until mixture is a fine powder.

QUICK TIP If you'd like a less spicy sauce, just use 1 Tbsp. of Italian Seasoning Mix.

make ahead

Prepare Italian Seasoning Mix up to 4 months ahead; store in an airtight container at room temperature.

Pizza Spaghetti Casserole

MAKES 6 SERVINGS   **HANDS-ON TIME** 15 MIN.   **TOTAL TIME** 1 HOUR, 10 MIN.

- 12 oz. uncooked spaghetti
- ½ tsp. table salt
- 1 (1-lb.) package mild ground pork sausage
- 2 oz. turkey pepperoni slices (about 30), cut in half
- 1 (26-oz.) jar tomato-and-basil pasta sauce
- ¼ cup grated Parmesan cheese
- 1 (8-oz.) package shredded Italian three-cheese blend

1. Preheat oven to 350°. Cook spaghetti with salt according to package directions. Drain well, and place in a lightly greased 13- x 9-inch baking dish.

2. Brown sausage in a large skillet over medium-high heat, stirring occasionally, 5 minutes or until meat crumbles and is no longer pink. Drain and set aside. Wipe skillet clean. Add pepperoni, and cook over medium-high heat, stirring occasionally, 4 minutes or until slightly crisp.

3. Top spaghetti in baking dish with sausage; pour pasta sauce over sausage. Arrange half of pepperoni slices evenly over pasta sauce. Sprinkle evenly with cheeses. Arrange remaining half of pepperoni slices evenly over cheese. Cover with nonstick or lightly greased aluminum foil.

4. Bake at 350° for 30 minutes; remove foil, and bake 10 more minutes or until cheese is melted and just begins to brown.

QUICK TIP We prefer turkey pepperoni, which doesn't give the casserole a greasy appearance.

easy side

Garlic Haricots Verts: Cook 2 Tbsp. olive oil; 2 Tbsp. balsamic vinegar; 1 garlic clove, pressed; and salt and pepper to taste in a small saucepan over medium-low heat 2 minutes or until bubbly. Toss mixture with 1 lb. haricots verts (tiny green beans), trimmed and blanched.

make ahead

Freeze the unbaked casserole up to one month. Thaw overnight in the refrigerator; let stand 30 minutes at room temperature, and bake as directed.

Cheese-Crusted Pizza Pot Pies

MAKES 4 SERVINGS   **HANDS-ON TIME** 30 MIN.   **TOTAL TIME** 50 MIN.

- 1 (12-oz.) package pork sausage links, casings removed, or ¾ lb. ground beef round
- ⅔ cup chopped onion
- ⅔ cup finely chopped carrots
- ½ cup chopped green bell pepper
- 3 cloves garlic, finely chopped
- 1¼ cups marinara sauce
- ⅔ cup sliced pepperoni (from 8-oz. package)
- ⅓ cup chopped pimiento-stuffed green olives
- 1 cup (4 oz.) shredded Italian cheese blend
- Vegetable cooking spray
- 1 (11-oz.) can refrigerated thin pizza crust dough
- 1 egg, slightly beaten
- 8 (1-oz.) slices part-skim mozzarella cheese
- Garnish: fresh oregano sprigs

1. Preheat oven to 450°. In 12-inch skillet, cook sausage and next 4 ingredients over medium heat 10 to 12 minutes, stirring occasionally, until sausage is thoroughly cooked; drain. Stir in marinara sauce, pepperoni, and olives. Simmer 3 to 5 minutes or until thickened. Remove from heat; stir in cheese blend.

2. Spray bottoms, sides and rims of 4 (10-oz) individual baking dishes (ramekins) with cooking spray. Spoon meat mixture into dishes. Place on a 15- x 10- x 1-inch pan.

3. Unroll dough on large cutting board. Cut in half lengthwise, then cut in half crosswise. Place 1 dough piece over meat mixture in each dish, overlapping rim. Brush with egg. Top each pot pie with 2 slices cheese, overlapping slightly. Bake at 450° for 16 to 20 minutes or until crust is golden brown.

QUICK TIP You can make these personal pot pies in ramekins, oven-proof crocks, or individual pie plates.

easy side

Parmesan-Romaine Salad: Whisk together ⅓ cup fresh lemon juice, 1 tsp. Worcestershire sauce, 2 pressed garlic cloves, ¾ tsp. kosher salt, and ½ tsp. freshly ground pepper. Whisk in ½ cup olive oil. Place 1 head romaine lettuce, torn, in a large bowl. Pour olive oil mixture over lettuce, and toss. Sprinkle with ½ cup (2 oz.) freshly grated or shredded Parmesan cheese, tossing to combine. Top with 1 cup large plain croutons, and serve immediately.

Tomato 'n' Beef Casserole with Polenta Crust

MAKES 6 SERVINGS **HANDS-ON TIME** 35 MIN. **TOTAL TIME** 1 HOUR, 10 MIN.

- 1 tsp. table salt
- 1 cup plain yellow cornmeal
- ½ tsp. Montreal steak seasoning
- 1 cup (4 oz.) shredded sharp Cheddar cheese, divided
- 1 lb. ground chuck
- 1 cup chopped onion
- 1 medium zucchini, cut in half lengthwise and sliced (about 2 cups)
- 1 Tbsp. olive oil
- 2 (14½-oz.) cans petite diced tomatoes, drained
- 1 (6-oz.) can tomato paste
- 2 Tbsp. chopped fresh flat-leaf parsley

1. Preheat oven to 350°. Bring 3 cups water and salt to a boil in a 2-qt. saucepan over medium-high heat. Whisk in cornmeal; reduce heat to low, and simmer, whisking constantly, 3 minutes or until thickened. Remove from heat, and stir in steak seasoning and ¼ cup Cheddar cheese. Spread cornmeal mixture into a lightly greased 11- x 7-inch baking dish.

2. Brown ground chuck in a large nonstick skillet over medium-high heat, stirring often, 10 minutes or until meat crumbles and is no longer pink; drain and transfer to a bowl.

3. Sauté onion and zucchini in hot oil in skillet over medium heat 5 minutes or until crisp-tender. Stir in beef, tomatoes, and tomato paste; simmer, stirring often, 10 minutes. Pour beef mixture over cornmeal crust. Sprinkle with remaining ¾ cup cheese.

4. Bake at 350° for 30 minutes or until bubbly. Sprinkle casserole with parsley just before serving.

QUICK TIP Whisk polenta while adding to boiling water and while cooking to ensure a smooth consistency.

try this twist

Italian Sausage Casserole with Polenta Crust: Substitute Italian sausage for ground chuck and Italian six-cheese blend for Cheddar cheese. Prepare recipe as directed, sautéing 1 medium-size green bell pepper, chopped, with onion in Step 3.

QUICK TIP Letting the meatloaf rest is the secret to clean, juicy slices.

easy side

Garlic Mashed Potatoes: Melt 3 Tbsp. butter in a saucepan over medium-low heat; add 4 pressed garlic cloves, and sauté until tender. Remove garlic from saucepan, and set aside. Prepare 2⅔ cup frozen mashed potatoes and 1⅓ cup milk in saucepan according to package directions, stirring with a wire whisk. Stir in garlic mixture, ½ tsp. table salt, and ¼ tsp. pepper. Let stand 5 minutes. Serve immediately.

Tried-and-True Meatloaf

MAKES 10 SERVINGS   **HANDS-ON TIME** 30 MIN.
TOTAL TIME 2 HOURS, 5 MIN.

2	lb. lean ground beef
1	lb. ground pork sausage
18	saltine crackers, crushed
½	green bell pepper, diced
½	onion, finely chopped
2	large eggs, lightly beaten
1	Tbsp. Worcestershire sauce
1	tsp. yellow mustard
½	cup firmly packed brown sugar, divided
½	cup ketchup

1. Preheat oven to 350°. Combine first 8 ingredients and ¼ cup brown sugar in a medium bowl just until blended. Place mixture in a lightly greased 11- x 7-inch baking dish, and shape mixture into a 10- x 5-inch loaf.

2. Bake at 350° for 1 hour. Remove from oven, and drain. Stir together ketchup and remaining ¼ cup brown sugar; pour over meatloaf. Bake 15 more minutes or until a meat thermometer inserted into thickest portion registers 160°. Remove from oven; let stand 20 minutes. Remove from baking dish before slicing.

METRIC EQUIVALENTS

The information in the following charts is provided to help cooks outside the United States successfully use the recipes in this book. All equivalents are approximate.

EQUIVALENTS FOR DIFFERENT TYPES OF INGREDIENTS

Standard Cup	Fine Powder	Grain	Granular	Liquid Solids	Liquid
	(ex. flour)	(ex. rice)	(ex. sugar)	(ex. butter)	(ex. milk)
1	140 g	150 g	190 g	200 g	240 ml
¾	105 g	113 g	143 g	150 g	180 ml
⅔	93 g	100 g	125 g	133 g	160 ml
½	70 g	75 g	95 g	100 g	120 ml
⅓	47 g	50 g	63 g	67 g	80 ml
¼	35 g	38 g	48 g	50 g	60 ml
⅛	18 g	19 g	24 g	25 g	30 ml

LIQUID INGREDIENTS BY VOLUME

¼ tsp	=							1 ml
½ tsp	=							2 ml
1 tsp	=							5 ml
3 tsp	=	1 Tbsp	=			½ fl oz	=	15 ml
		2 Tbsp	=	⅛ cup	=	1 fl oz	=	30 ml
		4 Tbsp	=	¼ cup	=	2 fl oz	=	60 ml
		5⅓ Tbsp	=	⅓ cup	=	3 fl oz	=	80 ml
		8 Tbsp	=	½ cup	=	4 fl oz	=	120 ml
		10⅔ Tbsp	=	⅔ cup	=	5 fl oz	=	160 ml
		12 Tbsp	=	¾ cup	=	6 fl oz	=	180 ml
		16 Tbsp	=	1 cup	=	8 fl oz	=	240 ml
		1 pt	=	2 cups	=	16 fl oz	=	480 ml
		1 qt	=	4 cups	=	32 fl oz	=	960 ml
						33 fl oz	=	1000 ml = 1 l

LENGTH

(To convert inches to centimeters, multiply the number of inches by 2.5.)

1 in =			2.5 cm	
6 in =	½ ft =		15 cm	
12 in =	1 ft =		30 cm	
36 in =	3 ft =	1 yd =	90 cm	
40 in =			100 cm	= 1 m

COOKING/OVEN TEMPERATURES

	Fahrenheit	Celsius	Gas Mark
Freeze Water	32° F	0° C	
Room Temperature	68° F	20° C	
Boil Water	212° F	100° C	
Bake	325° F	160° C	3
	350° F	180° C	4
	375° F	190° C	5
	400° F	200° C	6
	425° F	220° C	7
	450° F	230° C	8
Broil			Grill

DRY INGREDIENTS BY WEIGHT

(To convert ounces to grams, multiply the number of ounces by 30.)

1 oz =	¹⁄₁₆ lb =	30 g
4 oz =	¼ lb =	120 g
8 oz =	½ lb =	240 g
12 oz =	¾ lb =	360 g
16 oz =	1 lb =	480 g

INDEX

ISBN-13: 978-0-8487-4330-7
ISBN-10: 0-8487-4330-X
Library of Congress Control Number: 2013941127
Printed in the United States of America
First Printing 2013

Oxmoor House

Editorial Director: Leah McLaughlin
Creative Director: Felicity Keane
Senior Brand Manager: Daniel Fagan
Senior Editor: Rebecca Brennan
Managing Editor: Elizabeth Tyler Austin

Southern Living Quick Start Homemade

Editor: Allison Elizabeth Cox
Project Editor: Emily Chappell Connolly
Senior Designer: J. Shay McNamee
Recipe Developers and Testers: Wendy Ball, R.D.; Victoria E. Cox; Tamara Goldis; Stefanie Maloney; Callie Nash; Karen Rankin; Leah Van Deren
Recipe Editor: Alyson Moreland Haynes
Food Stylists: Margaret Monroe Dickey, Catherine Crowell Steele
Photography Director: Jim Bathie
Senior Photographer: Hélène Dujardin
Senior Photo Stylist: Kay E. Clarke
Photo Stylist: Mindi Shapiro Levine
Assistant Photo Stylist: Mary Louise Menendez
Senior Production Managers: Greg Amason, Sue Chodakiewicz

Contributors

Project Editor: Melissa Brown
Compositors: Frances Gunnells, Cathy Robbins
Copy Editors: Adrienne Davis, Barry Smith
Proofreader: Julie Bosche
Indexer: Mary Ann Laurens
Interns: Morgan Bolling, Megan Branagh, Susan Kemp, Sara Lyon, Staley McIlwain, Jeffrey Preis, Julia Sayers

Southern Living®

Editor: M. Lindsay Bierman
Creative Director: Robert Perino
Managing Editor: Candace Higginbotham
Art Director: Chris Hoke
Executive Editors: Rachel Hardage Barrett, Hunter Lewis, Jessica S. Thuston
Food Director: Shannon Sliter Satterwhite
Senior Food Editor: Mary Allen Perry
Deputy Food Director: Whitney Wright
Test Kitchen Director: Robby Melvin
Recipe Editor: JoAnn Weatherly
Assistant Recipe Editor: Ashley Arthur
Test Kitchen Specialist/Food Styling: Vanessa McNeil Rocchio
Test Kitchen Professionals: Norman King, Pam Lolley, Angela Sellers
Photographers: Robbie Caponetto, Laurey W. Glenn, Melina Hammer, Hector Sanchez
Senior Photo Stylist: Buffy Hargett
Editorial Assistant: Pat York

Time Home Entertainment Inc.

Publisher: Jim Childs
VP, Brand & Digital Strategy: Steven Sandonato
Executive Director, Marketing Services: Carol Pittard
Executive Director, Retail & Special Sales: Tom Mifsud
Director, Bookazine Development & Marketing: Laura Adam
Executive Publishing Director: Joy Butts
Associate Publishing Director: Megan Pearlman
Finance Director: Glenn Buonocore
Associate General Counsel: Helen Wan